YOUNG STUDENTS
Learning
Library®

VOLUME 11

HIV—
Jackson, Thomas Jonathan

NEWFIELD
PUBLICATIONS

SHELTON, CONNECTICUT

CREDITS

Page 1284 ZEFA; 1286 Louvre, Paris; 1287 National Gallery of Art, Washington, DC; 1300 ZEFA (top left and bottom right); Picturepoint (bottom left); 1305 ZEFA; 1307 Peter Willis Productions (top); ZEFA (bottom); 1308 Milbourne Christopher Collection; 1311 ZEFA; 1312 Paul Forrester; 1313 Paul Forrester; 1314 Robert Harding; 1315 Michael Holford; 1316 Royal Geographical Society; 1317 Library of Congress (top right); Armando Curcio Editore (middle right); 1323 The Mansell collection; 1325 The Bodleian Library; 1328 NOAA; 1329 Armando Curcio Editore; 1332 Images Colour Library; 1339 Idaho Travel Council; 1341 Idaho Travel Council; 1344 ZEFA; 1345 ZEFA (top right); Illinois Dept. of Business & Economic Development (bottom right); 1346 United States Public Health Service (top); The Bridgeman Art Library (bottom left);

1347 Mary Evans; 1349 Armando Curcio Editore (top right); National Gallery (bottom right); 1351 British Museum; 1352 ZEFA (top right); Washington Convention and Visitors Bureau (middle left); 1353 ZEFA; 1354 ZEFA; 1356 ZEFA; 1358 State of Indiana (top); Indiana Department of Commerce (bottom); 1360 ZEFA; 1361 Armando Curcio Editore; 1364 ZEFA; 1368 Sonia Halliday; 1377 ZEFA; 1379 United Nations; 1380 Frank Spooner; 1381 United Nations; 1382 ZEFA; 1386 Des Moines Convention and Visitors Bureau; 1387 Greater Des Moines Convention and Visitors Bureau; 1392 ZEFA; 1394 British Steel; 1400 Sonia Halliday; 1402 Sonia Halliday (top left); Museo Correr Venice (bottom left); 1407 Hulton Picture Company (top right); Frank Spooner (middle right); Columbia Records (bottom right).

Printed in the U.S.A.

ISBN 0-8374-9818-X

CONTENTS

▲ The Taj Mahal, built by Shah Jahān as a tomb for his beloved wife, is one of **INDIA'S** most magnificent monuments.

HIV

SEE AIDS

HOBBY

Any activity that is enjoyed during your spare time, and just for fun, is called a hobby. A hobby provides a way of relaxing and a change from your daily routine. Many hobbies that are enjoyed by adults were begun when they were children. Few people had much leisure time until recently. Now most people work fewer hours and have longer vacations than they have ever had in the past. They also retire at a younger age. Retired people are usually active and interested in many things. Hobbies can fill free hours and enrich a person's life.

Collecting Hobbies

Many children like to collect things. Bottles, buttons, butterflies, dolls, postcards, rocks, seashells, miniature cars—all these collectibles can make pleasant hobbies. You might begin to collect stamps after a postcard arrives with a stamp from a faraway place. You might find an old penny and begin to check dates on coins, then decide to collect old ones.

If you own a collection, you may want to display it so your friends can enjoy it, too. Hobby shops offer albums, shelves, and cases for orderly, attractive arrangements. Hobby exhibits and hobby books in your school or public library can give you information on caring for and adding to your collection.

Creative Hobbies

Many children like to make things with their hands, and so they take up creative hobbies. They might start by learning to weave simple potholders, and advance to making their own cloth or rugs. Or they begin drawing with pencils and crayons, and teach themselves to use paints. Knitting, dancing, music, photography, painting, and sculpting are some creative hobbies that can be done in your free time.

If you enjoy making useful or beautiful things, you can learn more about your particular hobby by visiting hobby shops, where they sell kits for dozens of activities, such as woodcutting, rug hooking, and model building. Museums, specialty stores, and church and civic groups often have arts and crafts shows where potters, carvers, weavers, glassblowers, and many others demonstrate their crafts and sell their wares.

Playing Hobbies

A third kind of hobby often grows from an interest in games and sports. Young people who enjoy tennis, golf, or skiing often continue to enjoy these sports for many years. Swimming, boating, fishing, bike riding, chess, and bridge are also hobbies of this type.

Part of the fun of any hobby is sharing it. The friendships that come when people share the same interests are another advantage of having a hobby.

Observing Hobbies

Another group of hobbies requires nothing more than opening your eyes to the world around you. Many interesting animals and plants can be found in every neighborhood. If you are interested in studying animal or plant life, you

▲ Chess, a game that can be played as a hobby or as a competitive sport, has been played for hundreds of years.

▼ Hiking in the countryside is an enjoyable hobby. You can see all kinds of interesting plant and animal life.

▲ This girl is playing a recorder. Playing a musical instrument is a fun hobby to pursue. You can join a band or orchestra, and get to play in concerts. Having a musical hobby is also a good way to meet other people who have the same interests as you.

Many famous people have had hobbies. George Washington studied the heavens through a simple telescope, designed furniture, and collected different kinds of tea. Franklin Roosevelt collected stamps; Dwight D. Eisenhower and Winston Churchill painted pictures. Churchill also loved bricklaying. There is a long wall on the grounds of his former home, built by the great man himself.

might start with trips to the zoo, aviary, aquarium, or botanical gardens. You can keep a record of what you observe in a notebook. You might draw sketches of some of the animals or plants you observe, and make notes about their habits. Library books can help you to identify the flowers, insects, and birds that you observe.

Many hobbies become the basis for enjoyable careers. Professional athletes often started enjoying sports in their free time as children. Inventors are often people who, as children, began to tinker with things that interested them. The best way to begin is simply by pursuing whatever interests *you*.

▶▶▶▶ **FIND OUT MORE** ◀◀◀◀
Collecting Hobbies see Autograph; Coins; Collecting; Stamp Collecting
Creative Hobbies see Carpentry; Carving; Clay Modeling; Cooking; Dance; Diary; Drama; Drawing; Enameling; Gardening; Knitting; Knot; Model Making; Music; Painting; Paper Sculpture; Photography; Sculpture; Sewing; Singing; Theater
Observing Hobbies see Aquarium; Bird; Butterflies and Moths; Chemistry; Dog; Geology; Physics; Rock; Shell; Terrarium
Outdoor Hobbies see Fishing
Playing Hobbies see Badminton; Bicycle; Boats and Boating; Card Game; Sports; Table Tennis; Tennis

HO CHI MINH

SEE VIETNAM

HOCKEY

SEE FIELD HOCKEY; ICE HOCKEY

HOG

SEE PIG

 ## HOLBEIN, HANS, THE YOUNGER
(about 1497–1543)

One of the greatest portrait painters of all time was Hans Holbein the Younger, a German from the city of Augsburg. He earned his place in art history by painting portraits at the court of the English Tudor king, Henry VIII.

Look at Holbein's portrait of a little boy, on the opposite page. You can sense from the painting, without looking at the title, that this was a very important child. He was the beloved only son of Henry VIII.

A court painter like Holbein had to get used to doing portraits of the nobles who were friends of the king. But what a problem this one-year-old baby named Edward must have been to pose! Holbein started with a sketch in colored chalk. Even in the

▲ A portrait of Erasmus by Hans Holbein the Younger, painted in 1523.

oil painting, he has kept the strong lines of the chalk drawing. Holbein's genius resulted in this handsome portrait of a future king in splendid, stiff dress. He holds his rattle as if it were a king's scepter. The other hand is raised in a kingly way. The portrait was a New Year's Day gift to Henry in 1539. He liked the picture so much that he gave Holbein a gold cup. The Latin inscription under the portrait urges the boy to imitate the virtues of his father. Edward never had a chance—he died at age 15.

Holbein was called "the Younger" because his father, called "the Elder," was also a painter. As a young man, Holbein the Younger went from his hometown of Augsburg to Basle, Switzerland. He was fortunate to be hired there to do a portrait of the great scholar, Erasmus. Holbein

soon decided to visit England, and Erasmus gave the artist a letter of introduction to an important man at court, Sir Thomas More. Holbein painted several portraits of More and his friends. Eventually, he became a court painter. Holbein keenly observed his fellow man, and painted his famous subjects with great skill.

HOLIDAY

A holiday is a day set aside each year for religious or patriotic observance, or in memory of a special event or famous person. Many people have long observed a "holy" day of worship each week. Sunday is the holy day for most Christians, Saturday for Jews, and Friday for Muslims.

▲ **The famous painting of King Henry VIII's son, Edward VI, by Hans Holbein the Younger.**

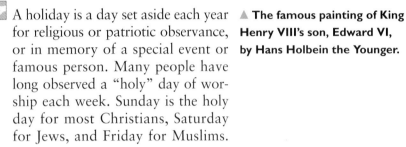

SOME INTERESTING HOLIDAYS		
Holiday	**Date**	**Meaning**
Feast of Lanterns	January or February	Marks the end of the two-week Chinese New Year Festival.
Abraham Lincoln's Birthday	February 12	Commemorates the birth of the 16th President, who ended slavery.
Shrove Tuesday (movable feast)	Last Tuesday before Lent	An occasion for merriment. In many places such as New Orleans, it is Mardi Gras time with carnivals and street parades.
Saint Valentine's Day	February 14	Marks the feast day of two Christian martyrs called Valentine. People send greeting cards to friends and loved ones.
Saint Patrick's Day	March 17	To honor the patron saint of Ireland. Irish people everywhere celebrate with parties and parades.
Good Friday (movable feast)	March or April	To commemorate the death of Jesus Christ.
Easter Sunday (movable feast)	March or April	To celebrate the resurrection of Jesus Christ.
Thomas Jefferson's Birthday	April 13	Commemorates the birth of the author of the Declaration of Independence and third President of the United States.
Pan American Day	April 14	Celebrates cooperation among the republics of the Americas.
Arbor Day	April 22	For planting trees. Arbor Day is observed by ecology-conscious people in other states on various dates.
May Day	May 1	To honor the worker with parades and speeches, especially in Europe. To welcome spring in the United States and England.
Mother's Day (movable feast)	Second Sunday in May	Celebrates the importance of mothers.
Flag Day	June 14	Commemorates the adoption of the Stars and Stripes as the United States' flag.
Father's Day (movable feast)	Third Sunday in June	Celebrates the importance of fathers.
Rosh Hashanah (movable feast)	September or October	Celebrates the Jewish New Year.
Yom Kippur (movable feast)	September or October	A day for Jews to fast and pray for forgiveness of sins.

▶ Independence Day celebrations on July 4 had already become a tradition by 1812. People gathered in the towns to celebrate with friends and neighbors.

FEDERAL HOLIDAYS

New Year's Day, January 1

Martin Luther King Jr.'s Birthday (January 15), celebrated the third Monday in January

Presidents Day, celebrated the third Monday in February, commemorates Lincoln's birthday (February 12) and Washington's birthday (February 22)

Memorial Day (May 30), celebrated the last Monday in May

Independence Day, July 4

Labor Day, first Monday in September

Columbus Day (October 12), celebrated the second Monday in October

Veterans Day, November 11

Thanksgiving Day, fourth Thursday in November

Christmas Day, December 25

When a holiday falls on a Saturday or Sunday, it is usually observed on the following Monday or preceding Friday

---

Sunday is also a *common law* holiday in the United States. This means that it has so long been the custom to rest from work on Sunday that people consider it a holiday.

Legal holidays in the United States are decided by the individual states. U.S. territories also decide on their own legal holidays. The federal government decides on holidays for the District of Columbia and for government workers. The governments of many states have also approved these days for celebration. Schools, banks, and many businesses are often closed on legal holidays. If a holiday falls on a Sunday, it is observed on the following Monday. The reason that some holidays are now observed on days other than their original dates is so that working people can have three-day weekends.

Many other holidays are observed in various parts of the United States. Other nations have holidays on different dates, because they observe different customs and historic dates.

▶ ▶ ▶ ▶ **FIND OUT MORE** ◀ ◀ ◀ ◀
Nonreligious Holidays see
Anniversary; Halloween;
Independence Day; Memorial Day;
New Year's Day; Thanksgiving;
Valentine's Day; Veterans Day
*See the table with the article
on each month.*
Religious Holidays see
Christmas; Easter; Hanukkah; Passover;
Yom Kippur

HOLLAND

SEE NETHERLANDS

HOLLYWOOD

SEE MOTION PICTURES

HOLMES, SHERLOCK

SEE DOYLE, ARTHUR CONAN

HOLMES, OLIVER WENDELL SR. (1809–1894)

Holmes was a medical doctor and a writer. He was born in Cambridge, Massachusetts, and was educated at Harvard College. He practiced medicine in Boston and taught at both Dartmouth College and Harvard. He wrote a very influential essay, *The Contagiousness of Puerperal Fever,* in 1842. It helped to convince doctors that they should *sterilize* (make germ-free) the instruments that were used to operate on people.

Holmes also wrote many nonmedical works. He published a series of essays in 1858, called *The Autocrat of the Breakfast-Table.* These essays revealed Holmes's wisdom and sense of humor, and they became very popular. Holmes wrote a number of other essays that appeared in the *Breakfast-Table* series, as well as novels and books of poetry. One of his most famous poems, "Old Ironsides," tells about the famous battleship U.S.S. *Constitution*, used in the War of 1812. Holmes wrote the poem to save the ship from being demolished.

HOLMES, OLIVER WENDELL JR. (1841–1935)

The son of Oliver Wendell Holmes was given the same first names as his father. He became a distinguished lawyer. He was born in Boston, Massachusetts, and was educated at Harvard College. Holmes served with the Union Army during the Civil War.

Holmes practiced law in Boston after the war. He edited the *American Law Review* for three years. He served, first as an associate justice and then as chief justice, on the Massachusetts Supreme Court from 1882 to 1902. In 1902, President Theodore Roosevelt appointed him to be a justice of the United States Supreme Court. He served there until his retirement in 1932.

Holmes was called the "Great Dissenter" because he often disagreed with the opinion of the majority of the court. He believed that laws should change as society changes. He favored legislation to improve conditions in society.

▷▷▷▷ **FIND OUT MORE** ◁◁◁◁
Law

HOLOGRAPHY

In 1948, a Hungarian-British physicist named Dennis Gabor (1900–1979) was trying to improve the photographs that could be taken by electron microscopes. He invented a technique that he called *holography*. At the time, holography seemed of interest only to scientists, but the invention of the laser in 1960 meant that holograms could become a part of our everyday lives. Maybe you have a hologram as decoration in your home, or have a book with a hologram in it.

A hologram is a two-dimensional (flat) object, but it shows a three-dimensional picture. If you move your head while looking at the picture, you can see the things in it from different angles, as if they were really there.

The light produced by a laser has only one wavelength, and all the waves are in step with each other. The light is all exactly the same color.

▲ Oliver Wendell Holmes Jr. continued giving lectures and publishing until he was in his eighties. He was, and still is, considered one of the great legal minds of his age.

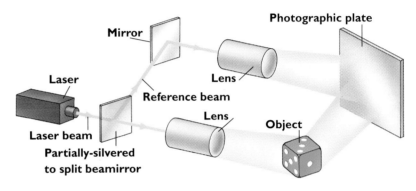

To produce a hologram, a beam of laser light is split into two beams that "interfere" with each other and form a complex pattern. This complex pattern looks like a jumble if you examine it closely, but it can be used to create the illusion of a three-dimensional object in the hologram image.

▲ Holograms are made possible by the highly organized light of lasers. Splitting the laser beam enables the photographic plate to record a three-dimensional image.

▷▷▷▷ **FIND OUT MORE** ◁◁◁◁
Lasers and Masers; Light;
Microscope; Wave

HOLY ROMAN EMPIRE

For many years, a large area of Europe was loosely united as the Holy Roman Empire. The area the empire covered expanded and shrank. But at different times, it included Germany, Italy, Austria, and parts of France, Switzerland, and the Netherlands.

The emblem of the Holy Roman Empire, the double-headed eagle, is one of the world's oldest symbols. It appeared on the banners of the Holy Roman emperors from the thirteenth century, and it can still be seen on the flag of Albania.

▲ The Holy Roman emperor had the right to be crowned by the pope in Rome, Italy. However, this caused some problems, as many emperors and popes disagreed with each other over questions of authority.

▲ A map of the Holy Roman Empire. The boundaries of the Empire were constantly changing. The Empire was officially ended by Napoleon I in 1806.

The first emperor of the Holy Roman Empire was Charlemagne, king of the Franks. Charlemagne conquered the lands that later became known as the Holy Roman Empire. In Italy, he helped to defend Rome against a barbarian invasion. In return, Pope Leo III crowned Charlemagne "Emperor of the Romans" in A.D. 800. In the 900s, a powerful German king, Otto I, gained control over all of Germany, Austria, and northern Italy. He helped the pope put down a rebellion in Rome and was himself crowned "Roman Emperor." The word "holy" was not added to the emperor's title until some years later.

The emperors were never able to capture all of Italy. A strip of land to the south of their territory was ruled by the Roman Catholic popes and was called the Papal States. The emperor and the pope were supposed to work together in friendship. But the emperors who came after Otto frequently quarreled with the popes. The emperors also struggled with the fiercely independent rulers of the cities in northern Italy.

By the 1300s, the emperors had lost control of northern Italy, but they remained powerful rulers of Germany and Austria. In 1356, the emperor decreed that his successors

should no longer be chosen by the pope and should instead be elected by a council of German princes. But until the 1500s, the emperor continued to go to Rome to be crowned.

Napoleon I of France defeated Austria and southern Germany in 1806. The emperor, Francis II of Austria, renounced his ancient title and the Holy Roman Empire collapsed. After his death, no more Holy Roman Emperors were elected.

▶▶▶▶ **FIND OUT MORE** ◀◀◀◀

Austria; Charlemagne; Charles, Holy Roman Emperors; German History; Henry, Holy Roman Emperors; Italian History; Roman Catholic Church

HOMEOPATHIC MEDICINE

In the late eighteenth century, the German physician Christian Hahnemann was trying to find out why a substance, quinine, helped people who had malaria. He noticed that if he gave quinine to a healthy person, the person soon showed the *symptoms* (signs) of malaria. He did more experiments, and decided that substances producing the symptoms of diseases could be used (in tiny quantities) as cures for those diseases. "Like cures like" became his motto.

He called his type of medicine "homeopathy" (*homeo* comes from a Latin word meaning "the same"). He said that his medicines were better because they cured the disease, not just its symptoms.

▼ This herb has been used for many thousands of years to bathe sore eyes and bruises.

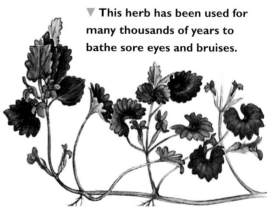

He was ridiculed at the time, but now homeopathic medicines are gaining respect. Many doctors use them along with drugs. For some illnesses they work better than drugs, and they have no harmful side effects.

▶▶▶▶ **FIND OUT MORE** ◀◀◀◀
Disease; Medicine

HOMER
(between 1200 and 850 B.C.)

A great poet named Homer was supposed to have lived long ago in ancient Greece. No one knows who Homer was or exactly when he lived. Many legends have been told about him. One story says that he was blind. Seven ancient cities claimed to be his birthplace. Homer's works may even have been done by not one, but several poets. The one fact that is known is that the name "Homer" has been connected with two epic poems of the ancient world, the *Iliad* and the *Odyssey*. (An *epic* is a long poem that tells a story of heroic deeds.)

The *Iliad* is the marvelous tale of the ancient city of Troy, its ten years' siege, capture, and final downfall and destruction. It tells of 51 days in the tenth year of the Trojan War, and of the quarrel between Agamemnon, leader of the Greeks against Troy, and Achilles, the greatest of the Greek warriors. The *Odyssey* is the story of the Greek hero Odysseus (also called Ulysses) and his travels. It describes Odysseus's adventures as he tries to get home to his wife and son. On his way, Odysseus battles with the forces of nature, savages, horrible monsters, and angry gods. The *Odyssey* shows Odysseus to be an ideal of strength, character, and heroism.

▶▶▶▶ **FIND OUT MORE** ◀◀◀◀
Greek Literature

HOMER, WINSLOW
(1836–1910)

The American artist who is called "the most American painter" was born in Boston, Massachusetts. As a young man, Winslow Homer worked for a publisher and created illustrations for magazine stories. Later, when he became a painter, he still liked to tell a story in his paintings.

Homer was a master at showing scenes from everyday life. He could capture movement and action in his characters against a background absolutely correct in detail. He has done this in *Breezing Up* (see below). How well he catches the sailboat in motion! Homer knew a lot about sailing, and has painted in correct details. The boy in the stern handles the boat by the line tied to the tiller, while the bearded fisherman is holding the mainsheet, so it can be let out quickly in case a sudden gust of wind comes up.

◀ **An ancient Greek coin depicting the head of Homer, the most celebrated of ancient Greek poets. No one really knows what Homer looked like.**

▼ ***Breezing Up*, a painting by Winslow Homer, can be found in the National Gallery of Art, Washington, D.C. It was a gift from the W. L. and May T. Mellon Foundation.**

LEARN BY DOING

Look at Homer's great painting, *Breezing Up*. It will tell you a story. Is it a good day for sailing? The artist's way of painting sunlight, clouds, and the colors in the water will tell you. How does he tell you where the boat is from? Have the boys had any luck fishing? How would you end the story? Try drawing a picture of your own that tells a story.

HONDURAS

Capital city

Tegucigalpa
(605,000 people)

Area

43,277 square miles
(112,088 sq. km)

Population

4,674,000 people

Government

Republic

Natural resources

Lumber, gold, silver, lead,
copper, zinc, iron ore,
antimony, coal

Export products

Bananas, coffee, lumber,
meat, silver, cotton

Unit of money

Lempira

Official language

Spanish

Winslow Homer was mostly a self-educated artist. After illustrating for several years, he became an artist-correspondent during the Civil War and visited the battlefronts. At this time he began doing watercolors and oils. Two years after the war, he went to Paris for ten months. Seeing famous paintings in European museums and the work of artists abroad made a great change in his style of painting. In 1875, he became the first well-known American artist to paint the life of the blacks in the South. An exhibition of these paintings was held in 1877.

In the late 1800s, the art of Japan was appearing in the Western world for the first time. Homer studied Japanese prints and imitated their flat tones, the grays and blacks with white accents against quiet backgrounds.

In 1883, Homer moved to Prout's Neck, Maine, a small town on the coast, where he could look at waves and rocks while he painted. He spent his winters in the Caribbean, where he painted many notable watercolors.

HONDURAS

In the early days of Spanish rule, gold mining was a major activity in Honduras. It is said gold was so plentiful that Native Central American fishermen used gold nuggets to weigh down their fishnets. Today, one of the riches of this Central American republic is bananas.

Honduras is slightly larger than Tennessee. Eighty percent of the land is mountainous and densely forested. The Caribbean Sea washes a wide coastline on the north and east, and the Gulf of Fonseca connects the southern coast with the Pacific Ocean.

Most of the people live in small villages in the western part of the country and on the north coast, where large banana plantations stretch along the hot coastal plains. Coffee grows along the cooler slopes of the mountains. The northeast, called the Mosquito Coast, is a wilderness of mountains, rivers, swamps, and jungles. Some native tribes live here, as well as in the southwestern part of the country.

Honduras has valuable deposits of silver, gold, lead, zinc, and oil and large forests of mahogany, cedar, and pine. But poor roads and railroads have hindered the development of these natural resources.

Most Hondurans make their living by farming. Some of them work for themselves, raising corn, sugarcane, beans, and rice. Others work for one of the large international fruit companies. Fishing and raising beef are important occupations, too. The Spanish-speaking people are mostly of mixed Spanish and native descent and they follow the Catholic religion. Just over half of the adult population are *literate* (can read or write).

About the time of Christ, several different tribes lived in Honduras. The most important were the Maya,

Map

CARIBBEAN SEA

Islas de la Bahía
Isla de Guanaja
Isla de Roatán
Isla de Utila

Gulf of Honduras

Puerto Cortés
Choloma
San Pedro Sula
Tela
La Ceiba
Trujillo
Tocoa
Olanchito
Arnan R.
Sico R.
El Progreso
La Esperanza Mts.
Laguna de Caratasí
Yoro
Chamelecón
Ulúa R.
COPÁN RUINS
Santa Bárbara
Humuya R.
Sulaco R.
Guayape R.
Catacamas
Patuca Mts.
Puerto Lempira
Santa Rosa de Copán
Gracias
Yojoa
Comayagua Mts.
Siguatepeque
Juticalpa
Patuca R.
Mt. Las Minas 9,347 ft. 2,849 m.
Comayagua
La Esperanza
La Paz
Tegucigalpa ⊛
Danlí
El Paraíso
Yuscarán
Coco R.

N
W E
S

Nacaome
San Lorenzo
Choluteca
Choluteca R.

Gulf of Fonseca

0   50   100 Miles
0 50 100 150 Kilometers
© 1994 GeoSystems, an R.R. Donnelley & Sons Company

who were fine builders and sculptors. Columbus discovered Honduras in 1502. In 1525, after 23 years of fierce battles with the natives, Spain claimed the country. Honduras, along with the rest of Central America, won independence in 1821, and became a republic in 1838. The Honduran government has been upset by frequent revolutions. It receives aid from the United States.

▶▶▶▶ **FIND OUT MORE** ◀◀◀◀
Central America

HONEYBEE

SEE BEE

HONG KONG

Hong Kong is a British dependency on the southeast border of mainland China. It is made up of the island of Hong Kong, Lantau Island, Kowloon peninsula, the New Territories on the mainland of China, and about 235 islets in the South China

▲ Chinese New Year celebrations last two weeks. Here we can see a dragon dance. Dragons are considered lucky in China.

Sea. The capital of the dependency, Victoria, is on Hong Kong island.

Nearly all of Hong Kong's people are Chinese, many of whom came to Hong Kong from China after the Communist revolution in 1947. Hong Kong has a warm moist climate but few natural resources and little farmland. Food has to be imported. Hong Kong is densely populated and is an important commercial and industrial center: Textiles, garments, ships, electronics, and plastics are manufactured there.

Hong Kong is a free port, having no import duties. It is also a popular destination for refugees looking for work. In 1990, thousands of Vietnamese refugees who came to Hong Kong were sent back to Vietnam.

European traders first visited Hong Kong in the 1500s. China gave Great Britain the island of Hong Kong in 1842 and Kowloon (with Lantau Island) in 1860. The New Territories were leased to Britain for 99 years in 1898. Hong Kong will be returned to Chinese rule in 1997. The economy of the islands is so different from that of China that Hong Kong will be allowed a period of 50 years to reintegrate itself.

▶▶▶▶ **FIND OUT MORE** ◀◀◀◀
Asia; China

HOOFED ANIMALS

Horses and other animals that today have hoofs, once had feet with five separate toes. But, over millions of years, animals started putting more weight on the middle toe, or two or three toes, which became shorter and stronger as the extra toes became weaker. Nails on the weight-bearing toes became thicker and almost encircled the foot. These nails are called *hoofs*. Hoofs are produced by

HONG KONG

Capital city
Victoria
(1,176,000 people)

Area
403 square miles
(1,045 sq. km)

Population
5,841,000 people

Government
British dependency

Natural resources
None

Export products
Manufactured goods, textiles, electronics

Unit of money
Hong Kong dollar

Official languages
English, Chinese
(Cantonese)

the skin, just like horns and finger-nails. Hoofs give animals greater speed, protection for the foot, and sharp weapons for fighting.

A horse, which walks on only one large toe, belongs to the group of hoofed animals with an odd number of

toes. Tapirs and rhinoceroses are also odd-toed—they walk on three-hoofed toes.

Another, larger group of hoofed animals walks on an even number of toes. They are sometimes called cloven-hoofed, because the hoof is divided, or cloven, into two parts. They include the pig, camel, deer, giraffe, cow, goat, and sheep. All hoofed mammals are *herbivores* (plant-eating animals).

▲ The camel (this is a Bactrian camel) has feet that are adapted to its way of life. It has very broad hoofs that spread to give it a firm footing on loose sand in its desert home.

▶▶▶▶ **FIND OUT MORE** ◀◀◀◀
Camel; Cattle; Deer; Giraffe; Goat; Hands and Feet; Herbivore; Hippopotamus; Horns and Antlers; Horse; Mammal; Pig; Rhinoceros; Tapir

HOOVER, HERBERT (1874–1964)

Herbert Hoover's years in the White House were the least successful part of an otherwise amazingly successful career. Probably no President ever began his duties with greater hopes. Hoover declared in his inaugural address that the American people were nearer to the final end of poverty than ever before. Yet only seven months later, in October 1929, the stock market crash threw the country into a panic. In the Great Depression that followed, many factories and stores had to close. Millions of workers lost their jobs. The conditions that caused the Great Depression had existed before Hoover took office, yet many Americans blamed him for their state of poverty.

The President himself had known poverty as a boy growing up in West Branch, Iowa. After his parents died, he lived with an uncle in Oregon and then worked his way through Stanford University in California. He studied mining and geology, and in a few years after his graduation in 1895, he was well established in a career as a mining engineer.

Hoover's work took him to many different countries. He was living in London, England, when World War I broke out, and he was in Belgium when it was overrun by German troops. Several million people were in danger of starvation, and the American ambassador in England asked Hoover to lead the Commission for the Relief of Belgium. President Woodrow Wilson appointed Hoover as U.S. Food Administrator after the United States entered the war in 1917. His job was to persuade Americans to raise and save enough food to feed the Allies and American soldiers fighting in Europe. After the Allies won the war, he took charge of the American Relief Administration, which provided food and clothing to Europeans who had suffered because of the war.

Hoover was appointed Secretary of Commerce when he returned to the United States in 1921. He held that post until 1928, when the Republican Party nominated him for President. During the Depression, President Hoover maintained that helping the needy was the responsibility of local and voluntary organizations. He believed that the federal government had no right to interfere. But conditions became worse, and he recommended a number of measures to Congress that he hoped would help. They did not bring the Depression to

▼ Public confidence in banks hit an all-time low during President Hoover's administration. By 1933, more than 5,000 banks had gone out of business, and 13 million Americans were out of work.

an end, and Hoover was defeated for reelection in 1932 by Franklin Delano Roosevelt.

But 31 years of service still lay ahead. Hoover participated in worthwhile causes and wrote books.

▶ ▶ ▶ ▶ **FIND OUT MORE** ◀ ◀ ◀ ◀
Depression

HOPI

SEE PUEBLOS

HORMONE

A person who grows unusually tall, say, to 8 feet (2.4 m), may do so because his or her body produced too much of the growth hormone. Hormones are chemical substances made in the body by *endocrine*, or ductless, glands. These glands produce and *secrete*, or send out, hormones directly into the blood. Hormones control the functions of cells and organs of the body. How fast your heart beats and how tall you grow are just two things regulated by hormones. Scientists have identified more than 30 hormones produced by endocrine glands in the human body. All animals and plants produce hormones, and scientists have learned how to make a few of them synthetically (in the laboratory). A person whose body does not get enough of a particular hormone may take that hormone in synthetic form.

One human hormone is *thyroxine*. It is produced by the *thyroid* gland, just below the "Adam's apple." It controls the way food is used by the cells. Too little thyroxine causes weight gain, because too much food is stored rather than used to produce energy. A person who produces too little thyroxine feels sleepy and moves slowly.

The *pituitary* gland, which is

**HERBERT HOOVER
THIRTY-FIRST
PRESIDENT**

**MARCH 4, 1929–
MARCH 4, 1933**

Born: August 10, 1874, West Branch, Iowa
Parents: Jesse Clark and Hulda Randall Minthorn Hoover
Education: Stanford University, Stanford, California
Religion: Society of Friends (Quaker)
Occupation: Mining engineer
Political Party: Republican
Married: 1899 to Lou Henry (1875–1944)
Children: 2 sons
Died: October 20, 1964, New York City
Buried: Hoover Presidential Library, West Branch, Iowa

Herbert Hoover was the first President of the United States to have been born west of the Mississippi River.

SOME IMPORTANT HUMAN HORMONES

Hormone	Gland	Function
Insulin	Pancreas	Controls the sugar levels in the blood and helps the body make use of sugar, which produces energy.
Adrenalin	Adrenal	Speeds up rate of heartbeat and breathing to support deep stress or high emotion.
Adrenocortical	Adrenal	Controls the level of water and salts in the body, influencing weight.
Cortisone	Adrenal	Active in breaking down protein in the body, a process as important to good health as the building up of protein.
Estrogen	Female sex	Controls growth of female body parts.
Progesterone	Female sex	Helps to prepare for and maintain pregnancy.
Testosterone	Male sex	Controls growth of male body parts.
Growth	Pituitary	Controls overall body growth.
Vasopressin	Pituitary	Increases blood pressure and regulates body fluids.
ACTH	Pituitary	Important in helping the adrenal glands to produce cortisone.
Thyroxine	Thyroid	Controls how fast food is used by the body, affecting weight and level of energy.
Parathyroxine	Parathyroid	Controls muscle movement.

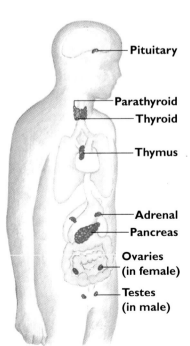

▲ **The positions of the major endocrine glands in the body.**

Pituitary

Parathyroid

Thyroid

Thymus

Adrenal

Pancreas

Ovaries (in female)

Testes (in male)

known as the "master gland," is situated below the brain. It produces several hormones. The hormones' main function is to control the hormone secretion of some other glands. The pituitary gland also produces the growth hormone.

Hormones can be sprayed on fruit trees to make them produce larger fruit. They can be given to animals to make them fatten quickly. Some scientists say that the meat of animals treated with hormones may not be good for those who eat it. Hormones may be used in medicine; they can help stop cancer cells from spreading. As people get older, they produce less of some hormones. This can cause diseases such as *osteoporosis* (weakening of the bones). People (mostly women) who have this are often treated with *hormone replacement treatment* or HRT.

▶ ▶ ▶ ▶ **FIND OUT MORE** ◀ ◀ ◀ ◀
Adrenal Glands; Gland; Growth; Human Body

HORNS AND ANTLERS

Hard spikes growing from some animals' heads can be handy weapons, or decorations to attract a mate, or plows to find food. These hard spikes are called horns or antlers. Most animals with horns or antlers also have hard coverings, called hoofs, on their feet. Horns, hoofs, and fingernails are all hard skin growths made of a material called *horn*.

Horns and antlers may look the same, but they grow in different ways. Horns grow from the skin. The outer parts of horns are made of hair growing together in a solid mass. Horns are usually described as hollow, but at the base is a chunk of bone to give them strength. They keep growing throughout the life of the animal, but are kept worn down by the animal's busy life.

Horns may look very fancy. Kudu antelopes, for example, have horns shaped like great curlicues. Antelopes, cattle, sheep, buffalo, and goats have horns. So do rhinoceroses and giraffes. Usually both sexes of these animals have horns.

Unlike the hollow horns, antlers are solid bone growing from the skulls of male deer as well as both male and female reindeer. Each spring the bone pushes its way upward. It is covered with a soft, furry skin, called *velvet*. The velvet contains nerves and blood vessels. During the growing time, antlers are sensitive and easily injured. As they grow, they branch out like tree limbs. In late summer, the antler growth is complete. The size and number of branches, called *points*, depend on the age of the deer.

When the growing is done, a ring of bone forms at the base of the antler. The blood supply is cut off. The velvet then dries up and gradually falls off. Male deer use their antlers to fight other male deer and win their mates. During the winter, the antlers break off and fall to the ground where they

◀ Stags' antlers can measure 55 inches (140 cm) and weigh 3 pounds (6 kg) each. The antlers fall off in the spring, but new ones grow quickly in the summer.

Rkhor

Oryx

Merino Sheep

▲ The horns of some animals, such as these, are very distinctive and decorative. Horns have sometimes been used by man to make drinking cups or musical instruments.

decay or are chewed on by mice and squirrels.

The *pronghorn*, or American antelope, has horns with a small prong pointing forward. These horns are shed and replaced every year, like antlers. The tusks of elephants, walruses, and wild pigs are extra-large teeth, not horns.

▶ ▶ ▶ ▶ **FIND OUT MORE** ◀ ◀ ◀ ◀
Antelope; Bone; Deer; Hoofed Animals; Skin; Teeth

HORSE

The horse is built for strength and speed. It is the most comfortable animal to ride. Horses have been domesticated and loved by people for about 5,000 years. Until gasoline engines replaced them, horses pulled carts and plows, and carried people in battle, in the hunt for food, in sport, and in their travels. Horses today are used mostly for pleasure and sport, but many of them are still used in agriculture and for travel.

Horses respond to love and careful training, but they react to their surroundings by instinct. Sudden movements or noise can frighten a horse. A horse defends itself with its strong teeth and sharp hoofs, and will run speedily from danger.

Horses are large, hoofed mammals. They belong to the family *Equidae*, which includes horses, donkeys, and zebras. Scientists know a great deal about the evolution of the horse. Its earliest ancestor was a small animal with several toes on each foot.

Horses are *herbivores*, eating only plants. Grass is the main diet of all horses, domestic and wild. Working horses need grain and hay added to their diet for extra nutrition.

A newborn foal has wobbly legs that look too long for its body. A foal can run at its mother's side a few hours after birth. Female horses usually bear young beginning at two or three years of age. Horses live about 20 years.

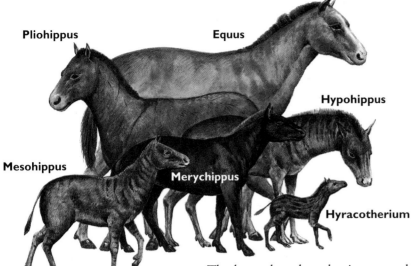

Pliohippus
Equus
Hypohippus
Mesohippus
Merychippus
Hyracotherium

▲ **Modern horses are bigger than their ancestors. The early horses have died out.**

QUIZ

1. To what zoological family do horses belong? Name one other animal in the same family.

2. The Latin word for horse is *equus*. What word, meaning horsemanship or to be on horseback, comes from this root word?

3. What is the oldest breed of saddle horse?

4. What are the two breeds of harness horses?

5. Are mustangs wild or tame?

(Answers on page 1408)

The horse has three basic, natural *gaits*, or foot movements. The *walk* is an even, four-beat gait. (*Beats* are the number of times one foot alone, or two feet together, strike the ground until each foot has been moved once.) The *trot* is a faster, two-beat gait. It is the trot that makes the clippity-clop sound of a horse in harness. The *canter* is a rolling, three-beat gait. The fast canter is called the *gallop*.

Terms Used With Horses

All baby horses are called *foals*. Up to the age of four, a male horse is called a *colt*, and a female is called a *filly*. After four, the female is called a *mare*. Adult male horses that can produce foals are *stallions* and those that have been operated on to prevent them from breeding are *geldings*. Most pleasure horses are mares and geldings. Stallions are usually used for breeding, racing, and horse shows.

Horses are measured by *hands*. One hand equals 4 inches (10 cm). The height of a horse is measured from the top of the *withers* (the hump below the mane) to the ground. A pony is less than 14¼ hands when it is full grown.

Some horses have two or more colors in their coats. A pinto, or spotted horse, usually has a coat with large patches of two colors. Roans have white hairs mixed in with hairs of another color. In one pattern, the horse is speckled and resembles a Native American blanket.

Most horses are solid colors. American albino horses have white coats, pink skin, and blue, yellow, or brown eyes. The palomino's shiny coat is the color of a new gold coin, and its mane and tail are silvery blond. The American albino and the palomino are colors, not breeds. Many horse breeders refer to them as *color breeds*. The Appaloosa, a color breed, is a roan with spots in varying patterns.

A bay horse is brown with black *points* (mane, tail, and legs). Brown horses have dark coats with lighter brown around the nostrils and eyes. A chestnut has a bright reddish-brown or flat brown coat, mane, and tail. Other solid colors include dun (dull yellow), sorrel (brownish-yellow), gray, and black. Many horses have white markings on their faces and white *stockings*.

Gray
Iron gray
Dun
Black
Bay
Appaloosa

Labels on diagram: Poll, Mane, Forelock, Crest, Cheek, Shoulder, Muzzle, Withers, Back, Croup, Haunch, Dock, Flank, Buttock, Gullet, Thigh, Stifle, Sheath, Gaskin, Elbow, Ribs, Belly, Knee, Chestnut, Hock, Shannon, Cannon Bone, Fetlock, Pastern, Coronet, Hoof, Heel

Breeds of Horses

Horses can be classified by type (light horses, heavy horses, and ponies), breed, or use.

SADDLE HORSES. There are several breeds of pleasure and general purpose horses. The spirited little *Arabian* horse, the oldest breed, is also one of the most beautiful. It has a short, compact body. The tail is held very high and looks as though it is floating. The Arabian horse has a face whose profile curves inward, a muzzle nose that is often small enough to fit into a teacup, large dark eyes, and an arched neck. It is gentle, spirited, and swift.

Morgan horses are all descended directly from a single stallion from Vermont owned by Justin Morgan. Morgans are lively and intelligent. Most of them are brown or bright chestnut. Their bodies are small and muscular. Morgans are used for pleasure, as farm horses, cow ponies, show horses, harnessracers, and jumpers.

The *Tennessee walking horse* is called the plantation horse because it was originally bred to carry Southern planters over their land at a comfortable gait called the *running walk*.

The slender *thoroughbred* originally came from England. Bred for speed, these spirited horses are usually ridden by jockeys in races. They are courageous, but skittish. Their necks, backs, and legs are long and packed with muscle. Thoroughbreds are often bred with other breeds of horses to produce some of the best horses for the show ring or the hunting field.

▲ Just a few of the most common points of the horse. Breeders and vets have a much longer list that they use for reference.

▼ Some examples of the variety of colors found in the different breeds of horses.

Palomino Skewbald Piebald

Liver chestnut Chestnut Strawberry roan

▲ **A highly trained Lippizaner horse. Horse and rider work so closely together when performing that they almost seem to be joined as one.**

▲ **Rodeos can be a fun family outing. People travel for miles to watch highly skilled horse riding, calf and steer roping, bucking-bronco riding, bull riding, and steer wrestling.**

The *American saddle horse* is usually seen in horse shows. These high-strung horses have rounded bodies and very long necks. The breed is divided into two types. The three-gaited type has a trimmed tail and a short mane. The five-gaited type is taught two gaits that are not natural for a horse. They have long, high-set tails. Ribbons are tied in their manes. They are sometimes shown in harness.

The famous white dancing horses known as *Lippizaners* are chiefly bred in Austria by the Spanish Riding School of Vienna. They have heavy, rounded bodies, yet they are among the most graceful of breeds. Lippizaners need strength and intelligence to perform the difficult, balletlike movements used in the performances.

The *American quarter horse* is the most important breed of cow pony. These stocky little horses are quick, willing, and hardy. They were first bred to run quarter-mile races. They have fairly short necks and legs.

HARNESS HORSES. The *standardbred* horse is a light harness horse bred in the United States for racing with a driver in a *sulky*, or cart. The standardbred's body resembles that of the thoroughbred. It is strong and heavy-boned. There are two types of standardbreds—the *trotters* and the *pacers*. The pace is an artificial gait, which the horses must learn.

The *hackney* is a heavy harness horse used in the show ring. Hackneys are trotting horses. They have a high snapping action in the trot. In the show ring the tail is trimmed and the mane is braided. The hackney pony is a smaller version of the hackney horse.

DRAFT HORSES. The biggest horses in the world are the heavy draft horses. They were once used to carry armored knights into battle. Later, they were used on farms and to haul heavy wagons. The five most important breeds are the *Belgian*, the *Clydesdale*, the *Percheron*, the *Suffolk punch*, and the *Shire*. The Clydesdale has the smoothest gait. It has long hairs called *feathers* on its legs. The Shire is the tallest breed.

PONIES. A pony is simply a smaller version of a horse. The *Shetland* is the smallest of all pony breeds. It can have a spotted or solid-colored shaggy coat. Shetlands have thick necks, stubby legs, and stout bodies.

The delicate *Welsh* pony looks like a refined miniature horse. It has slender legs and neck. Its sleek appearance and quiet manners make it

▼ **A Haflinger, with its luxurious straw-colored mane and forelock, is one of the most attractive horse breeds. It is a hardy, surefooted mountain pony originating in the Austrian Tyrol.**

LEARN BY DOING

If you live in the city, you might see a mounted police officer's horse, a horse being ridden in a park, or a horse performing in a circus. On the other hand, if you live in the countryside, you might see a workhorse pulling a plow, a horse running in a field, or one at a fair. Look at the horse's body, and watch how it moves. Try to name its color and breed.

popular. Welsh ponies were once used in coal mines to haul wagons filled with coal.

WILD HORSES. The only true wild horse living today is *Przewalski's*

◄ **Many generations of farmers have used draft horses to plow their farmland. Although sophisticated tractors and other machinery have replaced most of them today, there are still some working horses on traditional farms.**

horse. This small, rare horse is found in Central Asia in the wild. It has a rough, brownish-red coat, a heavy head, and a bushy mane and tail.

The American *mustang* is descended from domestic horses that escaped, so it is not a true wild horse. These horses still roam parts of the western United States, but the mustang population is decreasing every year. *Chincoteague ponies* live wild on Assateague Island, located between Chincoteague Bay and the Atlantic Ocean in Virginia. These ponies are also descended from domestic horses.

▶▶▶▶ **FIND OUT MORE** ◄◄◄◄
Albino; Donkey;
Equestrianism; Horseback Riding;
Horse Racing; Zebra

HORSEBACK RIDING

Since horses are no longer needed for transportation, riding them is chiefly for enjoyment. But in learning to ride, it is important that the rider show

consideration for the horse. Good riders treat horses gently. *Horsemanship* is the art of horseback riding.

A rider tells a horse what is wanted by the use of aids such as voice commands, leg pressure, and pressure applied to the bit in the horse's mouth.

Horses like to be talked to. A horse can feel the silent signals that the rider gives it by changes in leg pressure on its sides. The reins, which are attached to the bridle by the bit, are used to control the horse—to tell it when to turn and stop. Jerking on the reins and overusing them is a common fault of beginning riders. All the aids should be used, not just the reins.

Two main types of saddles are in popular use today. *Western saddles* are large, heavy saddles with a piece of leather called a *horn* sticking up in front to hold a rope. Most beginning riders like this saddle because it is comfortable and easy to sit on. The seat is deep. Western *tack* (saddle and bridle) is used on ranches, in parades, and in rodeos. Other riders prefer the *English saddle*, which is small and

WHERE TO DISCOVER MORE

Dell, Catherine. *Horses & Ponies*. New York: Random Books Young Readers, 1989.

Gise, Joanne. *A Picture Book of Horses*. New Jersey: Troll Associates, 1991.

Horses have very good memories. Their ability to remember a route home is said to have saved the lives of many a wounded cavalryman.

▲ **Several Plains Native American tribes, such as the Cheyennes, seem to have had a special relationship with horses. They tamed the wild horses which they depended upon for hunting and war.**

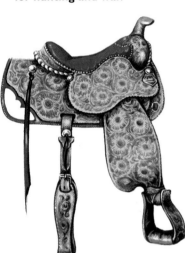

light. It has more padding in it, but it is flatter than a Western saddle and does not have a horn. English saddles are used in fox hunts, jumping contests, and races.

Riding clothing ranges from jeans to complete English riding costumes called *habits*. Boots with stout heels should be worn for comfort and safety. For formal horse shows, hunts, and other "English-saddle" activities, definite, standard outfits of clothing are required. Riding lessons are given at public stables, private riding schools, and camps. A friend who is an expert

rider can also be your instructor. No matter where you learn to ride, the instructor can teach you the right way to *cinch up* a horse (put on the saddle and bridle). The new rider learns how to *mount* (get on) and *dismount* (get off) the horse. Next comes the proper way to hold the reins. At first, the horse should be led around a track at a walk by the instructor. After the rider becomes used to the feel of the saddle and the movement of the horse, he or she learns to ride at a *trot* (two-beat gait or run), a *canter* (three-beat gait), or a *gallop* (fastest gait of a horse). In using an English saddle, the rider *posts* when the horse is trotting. In posting, the rider rises out of the saddle, then sits down again, in a continuous movement in rhythm with the horse's stride. With a Western saddle, the rider does not post, but sits firmly in the saddle.

Some riders using English saddles go on to learn to jump horses over fences and other obstacles. With Western tack, a more advanced rider learns *neck reining* (guiding the horse by touching the reins on its neck) and other techniques.

▶▶▶▶ **FIND OUT MORE** ◀◀◀◀
Equestrianism; Horse Racing; Rodeo

HORSEPOWER

SEE POWER

▲ **The ornate American Western saddle (above) is used for pleasure as well as for work riding. The all-purpose saddle (right) is better for a young rider.**

▼ **A diagram showing the rider's position and the action of the horse when jumping an upright fence. From left to right:**
1. The approach; 2. Taking off;
3. Suspension; 4. Landing;
5. Collection before moving off.

1   2   3   4   5

HORSE RACING

The exciting sport of horse racing is popular in many parts of the world. When most people think of horse racing, they think of *flat racing*—thoroughbred horses galloped by jockeys around a racetrack. But there are other kinds of races. In a *steeple-chase*, thoroughbreds jump over fences. In *harness racing*, standard-bred horses pull carts called *sulkies* around a track. Quarter horses are sometimes galloped in races with the riders using Western saddles.

Flat horse races can be of different lengths. Ten or more horses are usually entered in each race. In many states, people can place bets on the horses they pick to win, *place* (come in second), or *show* (come in third). *Purses* (prize money) are given for the horses that come in first, second, and third. Some horses have won more than $1 million in purses.

The three most famous flat races in the United States are the Kentucky Derby, the Preakness, and the Belmont Stakes. Horses from other nations are brought here to take part in races such as the Washington International. In England, famous races include the Derby (a flat race) and the Grand National (a race over fences). France's best-known horse race is the Prix de l'Arc de Triomphe.

At a race, spectators see *outriders* in red coats lead the horses out. The jockeys wear gaily colored shirts called *racing silks*. The horses are lined up behind the gate. A bell rings. The doors of the gate spring open, and the announcer calls, "They're off!" The jockeys maneuver their horses for the best positions as they gallop around the racetrack's turns. The winning horse is the first one to cross the finish line. Cameras record the entire race. A "photo-finish" photograph shows which horse's nose passed the finish line first if it appears there might be a tie.

▶ ▶ ▶ ▶ **FIND OUT MORE** ◀ ◀ ◀ ◀
Horse; Horseback Riding

▲ A special camera, aimed at a mirror by the finish line, shows the order in which the horses finish in a "photo-finish" race.

▼ A horse wears a light leather harness to pull a *sulky* along. The harness gives the driver control, although driving a sulky is not as easy as it is made to look.

HORSETAIL

A horsetail is a plant that has a jointed, hollow stem with a grooved surface. During cold weather, the parts of a horsetail that are above ground die, but the roots live through the winter, growing slowly underground. In the spring, new stalks grow from the roots. On the stalks are scaly leaves and cones, which contain spores that reproduce the plant. The cones break open, and the spores are spread widely by wind and water. In the right conditions, a new horsetail plant will grow from a single spore. The cones look like horses' tails, which is how the plant got its name.

All parts of the plant contain small crystals of *silica*, the same hard material that makes up quartz and is used to make glass. Years ago, horsetails were used for scouring metal; the silica acted as a kind of natural scouring powder.

Some horsetails look like small trees. Most horsetails are less than 3 feet (91 cm) tall, but hundreds of millions of years ago, horsetails in coal-forming swamps grew more than 100 feet (30 m) tall. The plant is related to *club mosses* and *ferns*.

▶▶▶▶ **FIND OUT MORE** ◀◀◀◀
Club Moss; Coal; Fern

The horsetail has two other names that are less well-known—scouring rush and pewterwort. These names came from using the horsetails to clean metals, especially pewter. Horsetails were also used as a *poultice* (healing pad) for cuts and wounds.

▼ The scaly leaves and cones of the horsetail contain spores. Can you see how these plants got their name?

HOSPITAL

A hospital is a place where people go if they need special care when they are not well. All hospitals have beds for *patients* (sick people). Doctors, nurses, and special equipment are also there to care for anyone who is sick or hurt.

Kinds of Hospitals

Some hospitals care for patients whose treatment takes only a short time—from a single day to no longer than a month or two. Chronic-care hospitals take care of patients whose treatment may take many months, or even several years.

In many parts of the world, all the hospitals in a country are owned and run by the government. In the United States, the Veterans Administration has a number of hospitals in which sick war veterans are treated. The Army, Navy, and Air Force have hospitals in which sick and wounded members of the armed forces and their families are treated.

Most hospitals in the United States are *community* hospitals, owned by the people of a town, county, or city. *Voluntary* hospitals are operated by religious or charitable organizations. Community and voluntary hospitals are non-profit institutions. Private, or *for-profit*, hospitals are run like a business to make money. *Government* hospitals are owned by the state or federal government.

Many people who are treated at hospitals do not stay in the hospital. These

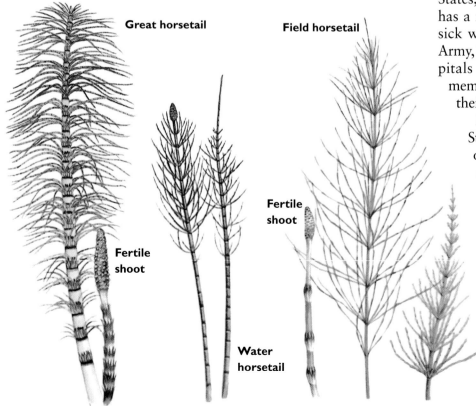

Great horsetail

Field horsetail

Fertile shoot

Fertile shoot

Water horsetail

people, called *outpatients*, come to a part of the hospital called the *clinic*. After each visit, outpatients go home. Other outpatients may just be treated in the *emergency room*. Patients who spend all their time during an illness in the hospital, living, eating, and sleeping there, are *inpatients*.

Hospital Departments and Their Staffs

People employed in a hospital do many different kinds of work. They can be divided into groups, or *staffs* of people, who work in various *services,* or departments, according to the work they do.

MEDICAL AND SURGICAL SERVICE. Doctors on the *house staff* (permanent or full-time employees) are divided into *interns*, *residents*, and *medical officers*. Interns and residents sometimes live at the hospital. An intern is a doctor who has just earned the M.D. degree and is getting a year of practical experience by treating hospital patients. Residents, or resident physicians, are doctors who have finished the intern year, and who work at the hospital to learn more about treatment in one particular branch of medicine. They also instruct interns, as well as medical students, who usually take hospital training in their third and fourth years of medical school. Medical officers are more experienced doctors who supervise the work of residents and interns, or who perform specialized medical work, such as surgery and psychiatry. Doctors in *private practice* (not on the hospital staff) make arrangements with a certain hospital to send their own patients there, where they can be cared for by both the private doctor and the hospital staff, if necessary.

The *nursing staff* includes *registered nurses* (R.N.'s), *nursing supervisors* and *nurses' aides*. Many large hospitals have schools for nurses. *Licensed practical nurses* (L.P.N.'s) do nursing work that requires less

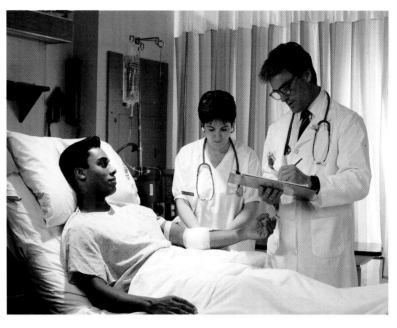

training than that of R.N.'s. Nurses' aides do jobs such as making beds.

The *medical and surgical service* includes the work of all these doctors and nurses (including students) in diagnosing illnesses, performing operations, seeing that patients get the correct treatment, medicine, and diet, and that they are comfortable.

FOOD SERVICE. The food service prepares the food for the patients and hospital staff. About a third of hospital patients need special diets (such as food with no salt or low fat). *Dietitians* plan the meals for each patient and see that they are prepared correctly by the staff.

LABORATORY. In order to diagnose a person's illness, doctors may require many tests to be made on the patient's blood, urine, and solid waste matter, and certain parts of his body. These tests are performed by *laboratory technicians* who work in the laboratory.

SCANNING AND X-RAY DEPARTMENT. Electronic body scans and X-ray pictures of the patients' insides are very important aids in diagnosing patinets' illnesses or broken bones.

MEDICAL RECORDS. Information about a patient's previous illnesses is needed to help decide on treatment.

▲ The medical service of a hospital—the doctors and nursing staff—work together as a team to treat a patient. They keep careful notes on all the patients in their care.

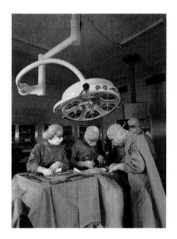

▲ A modern operating room, where patients needing surgery are taken care of.

The amount of time that people spend in a hospital is growing less each year. There are about five times as many out-patients as there are inpatients.

A daily record of each patient's treatment and condition is also important. The records of all outpatients (clinic patients) and inpatients are kept by the *medical records department*.

PHARMACY. Drugs, serums, and other medicines are needed to treat patients. These are prepared according to doctors' orders and are sometimes given out by the hospital's *pharmacy* (a drugstore where medicines and medical products are sold).

▲ Many modern hospitals have intensive care units where very sick patients are looked after. Electronic equipment is used to monitor a patient's progress.

The largest hotel in the United States is the Excalibur Hotel in Las Vegas, Nevada. It has over 4,000 rooms and as many employees to run it smoothly. It would take over ten years to stay in each room for one night!

REHABILITATION DEPARTMENT. Patients who have had serious surgery, such as a limb amputation, are often given special treatment by a *physical therapist*. The therapist is trained in methods of treatment and *rehabilitation* (restoring the patient to a condition of useful activity) without the use of drugs. For example, a physical therapist may help to heal an amputee's wound and show the patient how to attach and remove a *prosthesis* (artificial limb). Then an *occupational therapist* teaches the amputee how to walk or eat with the prosthesis. Occupational therapists may need to teach some patients new ways to dress, too, so that they can return to a normal life outside the hospital.

Being hospitalized may cause a hardship for the patient's family.

Social workers in the *social service department* try to help patients and their families adjust to life after hospitalization.

The History of Hospitals

Civilized peoples have had places to care for the sick since ancient times. These places were usually in temples, and the patients were cared for by priests. In Europe, the Church started and operated hospitals.

The first hospital in Europe was the Hotel Dieu, founded in Paris in A.D. 600. The first hospital in what is now the United States was opened in 1658 in New Amsterdam, which is now New York City.

In these early hospitals, diseases were easily spread from patient to patient. Patients were more likely to die in a hospital than if they had stayed home! It was only a little more than 100 years ago that medical scientists, such as Joseph Lister, Ignaz Semmelweiss, and Louis Pasteur, proved that disease is spread by germs. But most people did not accept disinfectants in hospitals until the late 1800s.

Today, people who plan and run hospitals try to make them clean, cheerful, and comfortable. Comfortable patients respond better to treatment.

▶▶▶▶ **FIND OUT MORE** ◀◀◀◀
Medicine; Nightingale, Florence; Nursing; Pasteur, Louis; Surgery; X-Ray

HOTELS AND MOTELS

More than 2,000 years ago, people traveling between the Middle East and Africa followed trade routes to distant places. They stopped at night near a spring or other source of water. Later, people built little shelters near the springs, and served food to the travelers.

These places became known as *inns*, the old Norse word for

"dwelling places." The French word for inn was *hostel*, and from hostel came our word, *hotel*. The first inn built in the American colonies was the Jamestown Inn in Jamestown, Virginia, established in 1607. Inns and taverns, or public houses for travelers and other people, were constructed along highway routes. A famous inn, the Wayside Inn, was built in Sudbury, Massachusetts, in 1686. It inspired Henry Wadsworth Longfellow to write *Tales of a Wayside Inn*. People still visit the inn today.

Hotels were built near other kinds of transportation routes, too. When lake and river steamboats became an important means of transportation in the early 1800s, inns were built near the docks. As American railroads spread across the country, bigger and better hotels were built near the railroad stations for the convenience of passengers.

Early hotels were uncomfortable. They did not have running water or private bathrooms. The only baths were in the basement. The first building in America built especially as a hotel was the City Hotel in New York City. It opened in 1794.

American hotels were the first in the world to have baths, elevators, public telephones, and electric lights. Some hotels built in large cities were luxurious. Few people could afford to stay in them.

Types of Hotels

The three types of hotels are called transient, residential, and resort.

Transient hotels are for people who are traveling for pleasure or on business trips. They are often built near major highways, airports, or train stations.

Residential hotels have people living in them for long periods of time. The apartments may have kitchens and dining areas. People pay rent on a weekly, monthly, or yearly basis.

Resort hotels are built near oceans, lakes, and in the mountains. People

visit them for rest, relaxation, sports, or entertainment. Some may open only during the vacation season.

Motels

People traveling in automobiles along highways began to rent rooms for the night along the way. At first, these places were called "tourist courts." Later, one-story buildings were put up where travelers could rent rooms and get meals, and where cars could be parked outside each room. These were called *motels*, a combination of the words "motor" and "hotel."

Modern motels, sometimes called motor courts or motor hotels, may be several stories high, with indoor parking lots. They are usually conveniently located along highways or at exits and entrances to expressways.

Hotel and Motel Operation

It takes many workers to operate a big hotel or motel. There are managers, advertising people, engineers, accountants, computer operators, laundry workers, electricians, carpenters, painters, desk clerks, cooks, kitchen workers, waiters, housekeepers, cleaning persons, and porters.

Charges vary in hotels and motels. In the United States, most hotels and

▲ **Motels are designed to provide convenient and inexpensive accommodations for people traveling by automobile. Many motels have good facilities, including swimming pools.**

▼ **The grand lounge ceiling in the Breakers Hotel in Palm Beach, Florida, is an example of the luxurious surroundings in many modern resort hotels.**

▲ **This dramatic poster was used to advertise an escape act by magician Harry Houdini. Crowds flocked to see his performances.**

▼ **How a house was built in the early Turkish town of Catal Huyuk. The walls were made of mud bricks. Instead of a front door, a ladder dropped through a hole in the roof giving entry.**

motels are operated under the *European plan*. This means that their rates cover only their rooms, and that the cost of meals is extra. Some resort and residential hotels and motels use the *American plan*, in which the rate paid by guests includes meals and rooms.

HOTHOUSE

SEE GREENHOUSE

HOT SPRING

SEE WELLS AND SPRINGS

HOUDINI, HARRY (1874–1926)

Harry Houdini was a brilliant magician who specialized in escaping from seemingly impossible situations. He was born Ehrich Weiss in Budapest, Hungary. His parents came to the United States when he was a child, settling in Wisconsin. He first worked as a trapeze performer, but soon started to learn magic. Houdini took his name from a famous French magician, Jean Houdin.

His greatest skill was escaping from locked trunks, handcuffs, straitjackets, and strong ropes tied around his body. He once had himself tied up and locked inside a packing case, which was bound with steel and dropped into New York City Harbor. Houdini freed himself in only 59 seconds. He always insisted that his magic tricks could be explained naturally, and he sometimes showed how they were done. He worked to prove that other magicians, who claimed that they had supernatural powers, were lying.

Houdini arranged a coded message to be sent to his wife after his death, in order to test *spiritualism* (the belief that we can talk with spirits of the dead). There is no evidence that any spiritualist ever received his message. He had a splendid collection of books on magic, which he left to the Library of Congress in Washington, D.C.

▶▶▶ **FIND OUT MORE** ◀◀◀
Magic

HOUSE

What sort of building comes to your mind when you think of a house? Modern Americans think of a building surrounded by a yard. But climate, available building materials, and local custom have caused houses to take many forms. In some parts of the world, people still live in caves. On the island of Rhodes, the Greeks built houses with few windows, while the Turks built light, open houses. Old Norwegian

Plaster

Mud walls

Central hearth

Sun-baked mud bricks

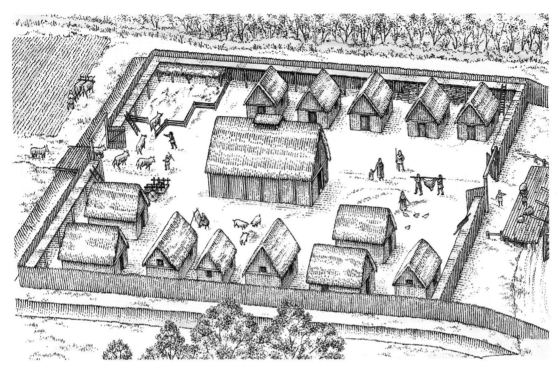

houses have roofs meant to hold the snow as a protective blanket, but old German houses have steep roofs to shed the snow. Front porches were popular in America in the 1800s for shade and breeze, but were not popular in colonial times and are seldom built today. In fact, in Europe they are very rarely built.

No matter where they are or when they were built, most houses have several things in common: places to sleep, rooms for work or play, storage areas for food and clothing, a kitchen, and some sort of bathroom. One room can serve many purposes. Through the early 1900s, many people took baths in the kitchen. Only rich families had separate rooms with bathtubs. Ordinary families would move a big tub into the kitchen on bath nights (usually once a week) and fill it with water heated on the stove. In the Middle Ages, people did not have our ideas about privacy. In castles, men and women worked and lived in the same rooms. Only the king and queen were important enough to have a room of their own.

Today, most of the family gathers together in a recreation room or family room. A hundred years ago, life was more formal in the house of a well-to-do family. Men had game rooms, and women had sewing rooms. There were parlors or living rooms for mornings, and other parlors for entertaining guests in the evening. Servants lived on the top floor of the house. In such large houses, it was not difficult to find a place to be alone. Modern homes are usually smaller, and sometimes do not have separate rooms for everyone to play or study in private. Every way of life and every kind of house has its good and bad points.

Houses in the Past
Before modern heating and cooling, house design had to try to protect people from uncomfortable weather. In warm climates, it was more comfortable in the shade outdoors than in the house. Houses were built around open courtyards in ancient Greece, Rome, and China. Cool winds could reach the outside windows and courtyard windows of these houses. In the shade of the courtyard, the family could work or play without strangers seeing them. Fireplaces were not needed for warmth—only cooking fires were

▲ Most Anglo-Saxon settlers built their houses and barns from wood and thatched the roofs with straw or reeds. Their houses could not last as long as modern brick-built ones since the wood rotted. Also, fire was a great danger.

The Hearst ranch at San Simeon, California is the most expensive private house ever built. Completed in the late 1930s, it cost more than $30 million and needed at least 60 servants to look after it!

▶ **A row of houses built in Amsterdam in the mid-1600s. Because building land was scarce, even the most expensive houses had to be joined in a row.**

▼ **A traditional Russian peasant's house, made of rough cut logs from the forest nearby.**

▼ **On this page and the next page are several styles of houses and apartments. They are from different historical periods and countries.**

Native American tepee

used. These climates usually had mild winters also. Portable *braziers* (open fires in metal baskets) were moved into the rooms when heat was needed.

In Arabic countries and in ancient Egypt, houses had to be cooled during the hot desert summers. Openings or wind scoops on the roofs of houses caught breezes and forced fresh, cool air down into the houses. During the hottest months, it was more comfortable inside these houses, even with no air conditioning, than it was in the hot sunshine.

In cold climates, a house had to be solid. Windows were small. Houses often had yards planted with thick trees that broke the force of the winter winds. Every room had to have a fireplace. Some fireplaces in the Middle Ages were big enough to walk into. Benches lined the sides of

these big fireplaces, and the family could sit inside the fireplace alcove.

People also saved fuel by enclosing beds with curtains that could be shut at night to keep out drafts. This allowed privacy for the people who were sleeping, too.

Until about 150 years ago, every prosperous home, even in America, had two or three live-in servants. Very rich families might have dozens of servants. Many servants were needed, because each family made its own food and clothing, or ran its own farm without much machinery. Houses had many separate buildings, such as barns for cows, stables for horses, coops for chickens, workrooms for weaving, and smokehouses to preserve meat. The kitchen was sometimes set away from the main house because of the cooking odors. George Washington's house at Mount Vernon, Virginia, is a good example of this kind of home.

Houses for rich families were usually designed with many separate rooms and areas. In China, men transacted business at home. A wealthy Chinese house had two or more courtyards. In the first courtyard, a businessman would work. In the other courtyards, the wife and children could play and work without being bothered by the office staff and visitors.

Modern Housing

Today's houses are generally smaller and easier to maintain. Modern equipment, such as central heating, air conditioning, and various electrical appliances add to the com-

Igloo

Hebridean block house

Indonesian stilt house

Mexican pueblo dwelling

fort of homes and simplify their maintenance.

A new kind of housing built today is *modular* housing. Modular housing units are built in factories. Separate rooms, and sometimes even entire houses, are moved to the building site from the factory and are put in place there.

Another type of modern housing is a *mobile home* (trailer). A mobile home comes on wheels, so it can be moved from place to place. To become a permanent home, its wheels are removed or covered. Then it may be set up on land often surrounded by other mobile homes.

Because land for housing costs so much today, fewer single-family homes are being built. Many people living in cities have homes in apartment houses. Some apartments have just as many rooms as houses, and are easier to maintain. People who rent apartments do not have to paint the building, cut grass, or pay for repairs. The building owner is responsible for this. Some people live in *row houses* or *town houses*, which are built next to each other. These homes do not have yards at their sides, though they may have front lawns. Some are built for one family; others, for several families.

Today, many people are living in *condominiums*, multi-dwelling buildings in which each unit is owned separately. Condominium owners share a common interest in the land and in the parts of the building used by all the residents.

English thatched cottage

Tudor house

Suburban house

Modern apartment building

▼ **The Xanadu experimental house in Florida could be the shape of things to come. It aims to combine convenience with maximum energy efficiency.**

HOUSE OF REPRESENTATIVES

SEE CONGRESS, UNITED STATES

HOUSEPLANT

The plants that grow in flowerpots in your home all year long are houseplants. A houseplant may be planted outdoors in the summer, but, unlike other plants, it will grow well indoors during the cold part of the year.

Kinds of Houseplants

Houseplants can be divided into several groups. *Foliage plants* are grown for the beauty of their leaves. Many have leaves with light and dark green designs, others have red or yellow markings. Among the foliage plants are ivy, ferns, Chinese evergreen, dieffenbachia (or dumb cane), aspidistra, rubber plants, and palms.

Succulents are plants having thick, juicy stems or leaves. These are good houseplants because they do not require much care, and they grow well indoors. Succulents grown as houseplants include small members of the cactus family.

Flowering plants have various flowering patterns. Some houseplants bear groups of flowers that fade and drop off at about the same time. Then there are no flowers until a new group blossoms. Other houseplants have flowers

▲ **The aspidistra is one of the easiest plants to grow. It used to be called the cast-iron plant because of its toughness.**

continually growing and fading. Among flowering house plants are the African violet, begonia, Christmas cactus, hyacinth, narcissus, geranium, and impatiens.

Plant Needs

Each kind of plant has special needs. Ask your plant shop for instructions for the plant you choose.

LIGHT. Some houseplants require a lot of light, some very little. Many plants grow best in direct sunlight. Place these plants in a window through which the sun shines.

WATER. All plants need water. Some can grow in fairly dry soil, and some need moist soil. Some plants need to have dry soil between waterings. It does more harm than good to most plants to keep the soil continually wet.

SOIL. Houseplants are grown mainly in one of two kinds of soil: humus or potting soil. You can buy bags of these kinds of soil in supermarkets or garden centers. By trying more or less water, you should be able to make your plants grow in any soil.

▼ **Two different ways of displaying your plants: hanging from a basket or trained to climb a pole.**

Hanging basket

Moss pole

HUMIDITY. Most houseplants can grow in the dry air of houses during cold weather. But, if your plant must have high humidity, it may grow better on the bathroom or kitchen windowsill.

PLANT FOOD OR FERTILIZER. Supermarkets, variety stores, florists, and garden supply stores sell plant food and fertilizer. All houseplants need one of these from time to time. To feed your plant, follow the directions on the package.

You may want to *propagate*, or grow new plants, from your houseplant. Many popular houseplants can be started and grown from a *cutting* or *slip*—a small piece from another similar plant. This cutting can be made to grow roots and become a new plant.

Place the cutting in a container of water so that at least one leaf node (the joint from which leaves grow from the stem) is under water. In a short time, the plant should produce roots and can then be planted in moist soil. Some houseplants, such as poinsettias and geraniums, can be put directly into moist soil to root. Plants that do not root easily can be treated with a rooting hormone, which is available from any florist and will help almost all houseplants produce roots.

◄ **Cacti are used to growing in hot, dry climates and should not be overwatered. This one is named the pincushion cactus for very obvious reasons.**

▶ ▶ ▶ ▶ **FIND OUT MORE** ◄ ◄ ◄ ◄
Bulb; Cactus; Gardening; Greenhouse; Plant

▼ **This begonia produces very colorful flowers. The stems can be very fragile.**

▲ **The partridge-breasted aloe needs a lot of light. It is an ideal plant to place on a sunny windowsill.**

LEARN BY DOING

Most plants grow well in moderately moist soil. The best way to keep soil moderately moist is to water the plants from the bottom of the flowerpot. You need a pot with a hole in the bottom and a wick—a glass-fiber wick (found in florists' shops) is best, because it does not rot. You can make your own wick, too. You need a piece of coarse rope, or a tight roll of burlap or part of an old towel. The wick should be about 3½ inches (9 cm) long. Push 2 inches (5 cm) of the wick into the empty pot through the hole in the bottom. Press the wick to the bottom of the inside of the pot, and fill the pot with soil. Place the pot on pebbles in a saucer, so that the part of the wick sticking out of the pot lies on the bottom of the saucer. Keep the saucer filled with water. The wick will absorb water and transfer it to the soil. In pots with no holes, place a layer of gravel in the bottom before adding soil.

▲ Samuel Houston, the Texan statesman and soldier who grew up with the Native American Cherokee tribe.

▼ Soil erosion, caused by flooding, can be seen all along the banks of the Huang He ("yellow river"). This soil gives the river its yellow color, which is how it got its name.

HOUSTON, SAMUEL (1793–1863)

The city of Houston, Texas, is named in honor of the famous Texas general and statesman, Samuel Houston. Houston was born on a plantation near Lexington, Virginia. After his father died, the family moved to Tennessee. When Houston was 16, he ran away and went to live with the Cherokees.

Houston joined the army in the War of 1812 and served under Andrew Jackson. Before the fighting ended, he rose to the rank of lieutenant. Houston became a lawyer after the war. He served Tennessee as a representative in the U.S. Congress for two terms. He was then elected governor of Tennessee.

Houston moved to Texas (then part of Mexico) in 1832. He later commanded Texan troops rebelling against the Mexican government. On April 21, 1836, he defeated a Mexican army commanded by the president of Mexico, Santa Anna, at San Jacinto. The defeat of Santa Anna made Texas an independent republic. Its voters chose Houston as president. In 1845, Texas joined the United States, and Houston went to Washington as a senator. He returned to Texas in 1859 as governor.

Two years later, Texans voted to join the Confederacy in the Civil War. Governor Houston was against this and was forced out of office.

▶▶▶▶ **FIND OUT MORE** ◀◀◀◀
Mexican War; Texas

HOVERCRAFT

SEE AIR CUSHION VEHICLE

HOWE, JULIA WARD

SEE WOMEN'S RIGHTS

HUANG HE

The Huang He River is the main waterway of northern China. It flows for more than 3,000 miles (4,800 km) and is the second longest river in China, after the Chiang Jiang River. (See the map with the article on CHINA). In Chinese *Huang He* means "yellow river."

The Huang He rises in the Himalaya Mountains of Tibet (now a region of China). Leaving the mountains, the river flows in a great bend to the north and east, skirting the Ordos Desert. For its last 400 miles (644 km), the river flows across a broad plain to empty into the Yellow Sea. It gets its name from the yellowish soil carried downstream.

The mouth of the Huang He has actually changed location. A century ago, this river emptied onto the East China Sea, south of the Shangtung Peninsula, where the river mouth lies today.

The sediment carried by the Huang He River builds up sandbars and makes navigation difficult. The Huang He is called "China's Sorrow" because of the many times it has overflowed, ruining crops and homes. For centuries the Chinese have tried to control the river, but have failed.

▶▶▶▶ **FIND OUT MORE** ◀◀◀◀
China; River

HUBBLE, EDWIN
(1889–1953)

Edwin Powell Hubble, born in Marshfield, Missouri, was a very important astronomer.

In the early 1920s, astronomers did not know there were other galaxies beside our own, the Milky Way. But they were puzzled by some odd cloudlike objects (called *nebulae*) inside our galaxy. Some of these could be seen as huge clouds of gas, but no one knew what others were. Hubble, working with the 100-inch (254-cm) telescope on Mount Wilson in California, examined the largest of these, the Andromeda Nebula. He found that it was another galaxy, hundreds of thousands of light years away. He also found that all galaxies are *receding* (moving away).

Hubble showed that there was a mathematical link, or ratio, between a galaxy's rate of recession, or speed, and its distance. This ratio, called *Hubble's Constant*, can be used to work out how far away the most distant galaxies are.

▶ ▶ ▶ ▶ **FIND OUT MORE** ◀ ◀ ◀ ◀
Astronomy; Milky Way

HUDSON, HENRY
(Died about 1611)

The Hudson River in New York State and Hudson Bay in Canada were both named for Henry Hudson, an English navigator and explorer.

Nothing is known about Henry Hudson's life before the year 1607, when he sailed northeast from England on his first expedition for an English trading company. He reached the shores of Greenland and Spitsbergen, but had to turn back because the ship could not go through the ice. A second voyage in 1608 also failed because of ice.

Hudson made a third trip, sponsored by the Dutch East India Company. His ship, *Half Moon*, sailed from Amsterdam in 1609. This time, when the ice stopped him, he steered west and south down the Atlantic coast of America. He hoped to find a waterway to the Pacific Ocean. He entered New York Bay and then explored the Hudson River as far as present-day Albany. By this time, Hudson realized that the river would not lead him to the Far East.

On his fourth and final journey in 1610, Hudson sailed on the ship *Discovery*. He was sent by an English company. The ship passed through Hudson Strait and into Hudson Bay. Hudson and his men spent three months exploring the bay's eastern shores and islands. Hudson wanted to stay there through the winter and continue the explorations the following spring. He and his crew spent a long, cold winter with little food, and many of the men died. The survivors became angry and *mutinied* (rebelled) on June 22, 1611. They tied up Hudson, his small son, John, and several other sailors, and set them adrift in a small boat to die.

▶ ▶ ▶ ▶ **FIND OUT MORE** ◀ ◀ ◀ ◀
Exploration; Hudson Bay; Northwest Passage

HUDSON BAY

Hudson Bay is a huge, nearly landlocked, body of water in east central Canada. Quebec lies to the east, Ontario to the south, and Manitoba and the Northwest Territories to the west. Hudson Bay is connected with the Atlantic Ocean through the Hudson Strait and with the Arctic Ocean through the Foxe Channel. The bay, including its southern branch, James

◀ **Edwin Hubble, the astronomer who studied many galaxies and found that they are all receding, or retreating, from us. He concluded that the universe is expanding.**

▲ **Henry Hudson explored the Hudson River in his ship, *Half Moon*.**

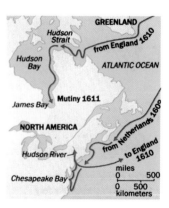

▲ **The routes of Henry Hudson's explorations. He was sponsored by both the English and the Dutch.**

▼ The coat of arms of the Hudson's Bay Company set up in 1670. It was formed to establish a fur trade in Canada.

▼ Fort Garry, one of the Hudson's Bay Company's trading posts. The company agents traded cloth and beads with the Native Americans for furs.

Bay, is about 900 miles (1,448 km) long and 650 miles (1,045 km) wide and covers an area more than four times as large as the Great Lakes combined.

Many rivers, including the Churchill and Nelson, flow into Hudson Bay. Ships navigate freely from July to October but are blocked by ice until well into the following year when the ice thaws. The bay was named for Henry Hudson, who explored it in 1610.

▶▶▶▶ **FIND OUT MORE** ◀◀◀◀
Canada; Hudson, Henry

HUDSON'S BAY COMPANY

Two Frenchmen, Pierre Radisson and Medard des Groseilliers, were interested in setting up a fur-trading company in the area around Hudson Bay. They could not interest the French government in their plans, so they went to the English government. The English were extremely interested. In May 1670, King Charles II set up a group of merchants called the "Governor and Company of Adventurers of England Trading into Hudson's Bay." This group established four trading posts on the west coast of the bay. At these posts, Indians could trade furs and skins for supplies. Explorers and traders traveled from these posts far into the interior. The fur trade was very profitable for the company. Eventually it established trading posts throughout western Canada.

The North West Company was an opponent of the Hudson's Bay Company until the two companies were united in 1821. Another opponent was John Jacob Astor's American Fur Company, which traded on the Pacific Coast.

The Hudson's Bay Company sold most of its land to Canada in 1869 for about $1 million. It continues to be the major fur-trading company throughout western and northern Canada. It also has a chain of department stores in Canadian towns.

▶▶▶▶ **FIND OUT MORE** ◀◀◀◀
Canada; Hudson Bay; Hudson, Henry

HUGHES, JAMES LANGSTON (1902–1967)

James Langston Hughes was a renowned black writer and poet. He was born in Joplin, Missouri, and studied at Lincoln University in Pennsylvania. Hughes worked at many jobs in the U.S. and lived in Mexico, France, and Italy. He spent a year of study in the former Soviet Union from 1932 to 1933 and was sent to Madrid in 1937 to report on the Spanish Civil War for *The Afro-American*, a Baltimore magazine.

One of Hughes's first published works was *Weary Blues*, a book of poems that came out in 1926. Besides poetry, Hughes wrote plays, novels, biographies, short stories, histories, and books for children. *Not Without Laughter* and *Tambourines to Glory* are two of his novels. Several collections of his stories about an amusing character named Simple have been published, including *Simple Speaks His Mind* and *Simple Takes a Wife*. Hughes wrote about his own life in two books, *The Big Sea* and *I Wonder as I Wander*.

Hughes's writings often showed the anger he felt at the unjust way that blacks were treated. But he wrote with humor as well as bitterness. Hughes received the Spingarn Medal in 1960 for his fine writing. This award is given each year to a black person who has made an outstanding contribution in his or her field.

HUGO, VICTOR-MARIE (1802–1885)

Victor Hugo was a French writer, best known for his novels *Les Misérables* and *The Hunchback of Notre Dame*. Hugo was born in Besançon, France. He was a brilliant child and won prizes for his poetry before he was 20 years old. His later work included poems, plays written in verse, and historical novels.

Hugo was involved in politics throughout his life, and he had to flee France in 1851 after taking part in a rebellion against Louis Napoleon. He went to live on Guernsey, an island in the English Channel, in 1855. By 1862, Hugo's writings had won him worldwide fame. He returned to France in 1870.

Hugo's imaginative, romantic, and emotional writing influenced other writers for many years after his death.

The Hunchback of Notre Dame is a gripping story of the pathetic Quasimodo, a hunchback who was the bell ringer in the Cathedral of Notre Dame in Paris during the 1400s. The book also tells much about how people lived in those days.

Les Misérables, published in 1862, tells the bitter tale of an ex-convict who had stolen some bread, and was chased through the sewers of Paris by a vengeful policeman. *Les Misérables* has been turned into a dramatic and highly successful musical.

HUMAN BEING

Where did people come from? How did people get to be the way they are? Humanity, or mankind, is several million years old. Men and women who lived in prehistoric times wrote no history books, but they did leave a record of themselves and their way of life. There are scientists who study this record of prehistoric human beings. *Archaeologists* study the remains of cultures from paintings to trash heaps. *Physical anthropologists* study the way human beings looked in the past, the way they look now, and how they have changed. Physical anthropologists look at fossil bones and teeth to find out what prehistoric people looked like.

The Earliest Beginnings

In the 1930s, an archaeologist digging in the hills of India found a jawbone and teeth belonging to a very ancient type of ape. Scientists believed the fossil was about 14 million years old, but it was shaped like a human being's jawbone! All the teeth in this jawbone were about the same size. This is not the case with the jawbones of apes and monkeys. They have sharp eyeteeth (*canines*) for ripping food apart and for biting attackers.

Scientists decided that this ancient jawbone must belong to a kind of ape they had not known about before. They called this ape *Ramapithecus*. Ramapithecus probably died out about ten million years ago.

Only small fragments of Ramapithecus fossil skeletons have been found. No leg, hip, or spine bones are known. Such bones would show if Ramapithecus could stand up, like a person, or only try to, like an ape. Monkeys and apes can move around on their hind legs, but not for long. Their bodies are not built for standing upright on two feet. Human beings

▲ James Langston Hughes, American novelist, playwright, and poet.

◄ *Dryopithecus* is the creature likely to have been the ancestor of modern apes.

▼ Victor Hugo, famous French writer.

▼ *Australopithecus* lived in Africa two million years ago. These early humans still had apelike faces, but their brains had grown a little larger. They could walk fully upright.

are the only mammals whose bodies are built for walking around on two feet all the time.

The Ape That Walked

Archaeologists and anthropologists working in Africa during this century have discovered some very ancient bones believed to be about one to three million years old. One skull, called *Skull 1470*, was discovered in 1972 by Richard Leakey. It dates from about 2.6 million years ago, and is very much like the skull of a modern person. Some experts think that people of this type were our ancestors.

Slightly more recent than Skull 1470 are some other fossil apes. These apes seem to have been able to walk upright on two feet. Their teeth were not very different from human teeth. This type of ape is called *Australopithecus*.

Australopithecus did not live in trees, like monkeys, but instead roamed on the ground. The change from tree to ground living took a very long time to occur. Scientists believe that millions of years ago,

Europe, Asia, and Africa were mostly hot, tropical forests and jungles. In some places apes could find more food on the ground than in the trees. If the food remained plentiful year after year, the apes best able to stay on the ground would spend more and more time there.

This is probably how Australopithecus changed from a tree-ape to a ground-ape and began to stand upright. Apes have good eyesight to help them when moving from branch to branch, and they use their hands for grasping and picking food from the trees. The apes that searched for food on the ground began to use their hands in new and different ways. They began to use tools to help them find food—a stick to dig for insects or a stone to kill a small animal. Because the ground-apes stood upright, they could also use tools as weapons.

To make the tools, australopithecines had to *think* about how to do it. They had to *experiment* with their hands. Hands, tools, thinking, and standing upright all worked together to make a more intelligent and adaptable creature.

This is how many scientists believe Australopithecus evolved from a tree-ape. Other scientists wonder if the development of intelligence had something to do with the beginning of the most recent (*Pleistocene*) ice age. Perhaps, when the climate got much colder and there was much less food to be found, only the more intelligent ground-apes survived to mate and so produce intelligent offspring. In this model of how things happened, intelligence was a *survival characteristic*. In other words, the more intelligent apes survived and the less intelligent ones died.

Archaeologists in Africa have discovered very crude tools that they think australopithecines made by chipping stones to make them sharper. As these beings became more intelligent, they also grew larger and more powerful. Archaeologists think

CLASSIFICATION OF A HUMAN BEING	
Kingdom	Animalia
Phylum	Vertebrata
Class	Mammalia
Order	Primata
Family	Hominidae
Genus	Homo
Species	Sapiens

that finally they became so much like a person that they could properly be called a human type rather than an ape. However, it is not certain that the australopithecines were our ancestors. Many scientists now believe that this intelligent, human-like ape died out. They believe that apes of the Skull 1470 type evolved in the same way as the australopithecines, and that it was this *strain*, or type, that led to humankind.

The First True Human Being

The next known type of prehistoric human being is called *Homo erectus* meaning "standing man." (This type used to be called *Pithecanthropus erectus*.) The earliest fossils of Homo erectus date from as much as 1.9 million years ago; the most recent from 200,000 years ago. The body of Homo erectus looked much like ours, but its face was made up of very heavy bones. It had hardly any chin. Its forehead was quite small and sloped directly back from the eyebrows, which were thick and heavy. Its brain was larger than that of Australopithecus.

Homo erectus could walk better than Australopithecus. The australo-pithecines' leg and hip bones show that they could run well, but that they walked with their feet turned out, in a kind of waddle, swaying from side to side. The leg and hip bones of Homo erectus are much like a modern person's, and show that these people were excellent walkers.

Archaeologists have found bits of burned wood and bones in the caves where Homo erectus sometimes lived. These show that Homo erectus knew how to use fire. Perhaps they saw the fires caused by lightning, and started to save burning branches.

Scientists think that Homo erectus had some sort of speech. Language was probably necessary for teaching children how to make the more complicated tools and how to make fire. Language was probably needed, too, for planning hunts. Homo erectus had a brain large enough to do most of what a modern person can do.

Neanderthal Man

The first prehistoric skull ever found that was thought to belong to a human was that of Neanderthal Man (*Homo neanderthalensis*), who lived about 110,000 to 35,000 years ago. Neanderthal people were skilled

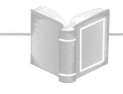

▲ *Homo erectus* is known to have lived in many parts of the world. In China, "Peking man" lived in caves and made a variety of tools for hunting.

WHERE TO DISCOVER MORE

Caselli, Giovanni. *The Everyday Life of an Ice Age Hunter.* New York: Peter Bedrick Books Inc., 1992.

Coville, Bruce. *Prehistoric People.* New York: Doubleday, 1990.

◄ Neanderthal hunters wore animal skins to keep warm. They were very much like people today, although they were more heavily built.

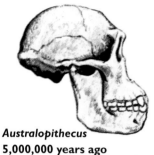

Australopithecus
5,000,000 years ago

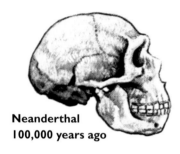

Homo erectus
1,000,000 years ago

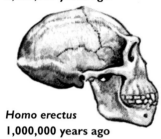

Neanderthal
100,000 years ago

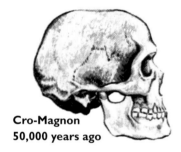

Cro-Magnon
50,000 years ago

▲ Changes in the shape of the human skull, as shown in fossil remains, help experts trace the history of man.

hunters and ate a great variety of animals—from mice to *mammoths* (huge woolly elephants, now extinct). They used fire a lot and even dug shallow hearths in caves. Not all Neanderthals lived in caves; some preferred tents made of animal skins and tree branches. Neanderthals made tools of all kinds—axes, knives, choppers, scrapers, saws, chisels, planes, and tools for punching holes.

The face of a Neanderthal was similar to that of Homo erectus. However, in some parts of the world Neanderthal skulls with bigger foreheads have been found. Neanderthals had a heavy, overhanging brow that connected in a ridge over the nose. These people were short—about 5 feet (1.5 m) tall—but they were strongly built and powerful, though somewhat bowlegged. They were the first people to start using decorations; they made designs on stones and on bones. They also polished stones for jewelry. They were the first human beings we know who buried their dead in graves.

Surprisingly, the brain of a Neanderthal was actually *bigger* than that of a modern person.

Cro-Magnon Man

However, Neanderthal people did not survive. They were either absorbed or annihilated by a new type of early human, Cro-Magnon Man (named for the Cro-Magnon cave in France, where fossil remains

were first found). Cro-Magnon people thrived about 35,000 and 10,000 years ago. They looked very much like modern human beings, and so are classified in the same species as we are: *Homo sapiens* (thinking man). These people were extremely skilled hunters, and made many different types of tools. They invented the needle with an eye, and began to sew clothes from skins.

The most remarkable skill Cro-Magnon people developed was that of painting. Deep in caves in France and Spain, archaeologists have discovered enormous paintings of animals and humans on the walls. It is thought that these paintings were used as a form of magic, to bring success to hunters.

Cro-Magnon people also made tiny statues of women that they put in their living places. These were probably meant to represent fertility goddesses, who would ensure plentiful food and numerous children.

The Cro-Magnons lived in caves or in small huts made of skins and branches. When the weather became cold and windy, they lived in shallow pits in the ground that they also covered with skins and branches. They learned how to store food. This was especially important in the winter, when animals were scarce and not much hunting could be done. When good weather came, the people picked up their belongings and traveled in search of animals for food.

Modern Human Beings

The greatest change in the human way of life probably happened about 12,000 years ago. People learned to domesticate plants and animals for food. They no longer needed to go hunting. They learned how to plant seeds to make crops grow, and how to tame and keep animals. For the first time, people started *producing* their own food instead of *gathering* or *hunting* it.

This made a significant change in

AUSTRALOPITHECUS

The jaw of *Australopithecus* is midway between the jaw of a modern ape and a modern human. *Australopithecus* did not have the large fangs that apes have today, but its other teeth were still large.

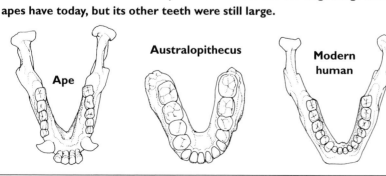

Ape

Australopithecus

Modern human

◀ About 20,000 years ago, modern humans lived in caves or huts made from wood and animal skins. They made tools of stone or bone to prepare their food.

the way people lived. When human beings were food-gatherers, they had to live in very small groups and always be ready to move on, to find more animals and grains to eat.

However, once people became food-producers, they lived in one place all the time, because they could not wander far from their crops and animals. They could store food and own more things, because they stayed in one place. There was more time to develop *civilization*.

People settled down and began to form villages. People who lived together in one place had to agree on rules for getting along with each other. This was the beginning of *law*. People in different villages began to *trade* with each other. Stone tools were replaced with tools of bronze and then iron. Some villages grew until they became *towns* or *cities*. *Nations* came into being, with definite areas of land ruled by a single leader. Writing was invented as a way to keep records of what people were doing and thinking.

Races

People speak of "races," but it is hard to say exactly what a race *is*. Races, whether they are of animals or plants, are groups that are slightly different from other groups in the same *species*. Races of people differ in how often certain genes occur—

genes that control the color of eyes and skin and the texture of hair, for example. People from different races are different in a few ways, but they are alike in millions of ways. In fact, it is difficult to distinguish races within the human species; for example, a classification done by color differs from one done by blood-group.

It is easier to talk of *ethnic groups*. An ethnic group is a number of people who share the same religious and cultural background. Most ethnic groups work well with each other, respecting their differences and trying to understand each other.

▶▶▶▶ **FIND OUT MORE** ◀◀◀◀
Human Body see Brain; Eye; Food; Hands and Feet; Skeleton; Teeth
Human Civilization see Agriculture; Ancient Civilizations; Art History; Burial Customs; City; Civilization; Culture; Law; Prehistory; Religion; Science; Written Language
Human Environment see Cave Dwellers; Folsom Culture; Ice Age; Lake Dwellers; Mammals of the Past; Stone Age
Human Evolution see Anthropology; Ape; Archeology; Darwin, Charles; Evolution; Fossil; Leakey Family; Monkey
Human Mind see Brain; Freud, Sigmund; Intelligence; Jung, Carl; Learning; Psychology

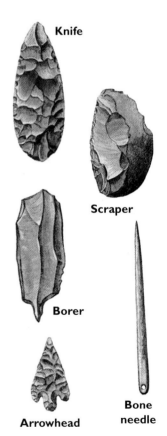

Knife

Scraper

Borer

Arrowhead

Bone needle

▲ Flint was often used for making tools. Early humans also made needles from bone.

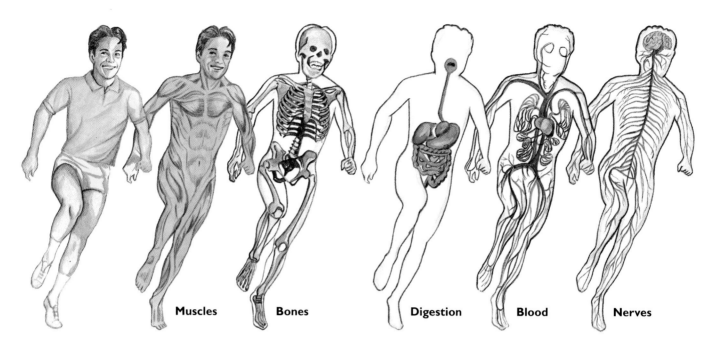

Muscles Bones Digestion Blood Nerves

▲ The body works through a series of interconnected systems that function all the time to keep us going.

The normal pulse rate is 60 to 90 beats a minute. In the course of an average lifetime, and without any servicing, the heart beats some 2,500,000,000 times. Our blood takes one minute to leave the heart, flow through the body and return.

HUMAN BODY

Your body is made up of many parts. Each part has a special job, but all the parts work together. Your body, like a machine, needs fuel to give it energy. The fuel your body uses is food. The oxygen contained in the air you breathe helps to turn the food you eat, and digest, into energy.

Cells and Organs

Living things—both plants and animals—are made up of *cells*. Cells are the basic units of life. The human body is made up of billions of cells of many different kinds. Growth of the body is caused by an increase in the number of cells. Cells are always growing, dying, and being replaced.

A group of cells of the same kind that perform a particular task is called a *tissue*. For example, cells that shorten and lengthen are collected in muscle tissue. Cells that transmit nervous impulses form nervous tissue. Tissues of different kinds make up an *organ*. An organ is a unit of the body that has a specific function, or job. The eye is an organ. The heart is an organ with the task of pumping blood. Other organs are the lungs, liver, tongue, and stomach.

The skin is the largest organ of your body. The skin protects the body and gives it an airtight and waterproof covering. It also keeps out bacteria that cause infections. The skin gets rid of some of the body's wastes, in the form of perspiration. It also helps to keep the temperature of the body constant.

The structure of the skin is seen by using a microscope. Skin is made up of two basic layers. The outer layer is the *epidermis*. It is made up of dead, flattened cells that wear off. Blood vessels, nerves, sweat and oil glands, lymph spaces, and tiny muscles are in the inner layer of the skin, the *dermis*. Nails grow from the dermis.

The organs of the body work together in groups called *systems*. The *digestive system* (mouth, teeth, stomach, and intestines) has the job of changing food into a form that can be used by the cells. The *circulatory system* (heart, veins, and arteries) carries substances, such as food and gases, to and from the cells of the body.

The *nervous system* (brain, spinal cord, and network of nerve cells) controls and coordinates not only the digestive and circulatory systems, but also all the other systems and parts of the body. Nerve cells carry "messages" back and forth between the brain and the rest of the body.

Anatomy is the study of the structure of the body's systems. The way in which the systems work is studied in *physiology*. *Biochemistry* covers the chemical reactions that take place in each system.

☀ HUMBOLDT, ALEXANDER VON (1769–1859)

The German scientist Alexander von Humboldt was interested in geography and many other sciences. He wrote a huge encyclopedia of the natural world, called *Kosmos*, and today he is recognized as the founder of the modern sciences of physical geography and geophysics.

Humboldt was born in Berlin, Germany. He traveled widely throughout Europe and Central and South America. With his French companion, Aimé Bonpland, he explored the dense rain forests of the Amazon and Orinoco river basins, studying animals and plants. He climbed to a height of 18,893 feet (5,759 m) on the volcanic peak of Chimborazo in Ecuador. In 1802, when Humboldt made this climb, no one before had ever climbed so high up a mountain.

Humboldt was also interested in the ocean. He charted the ocean current off the coast of western South America that today bears his name. His observations of the weather helped improve methods of weather forecasting. Everything he saw on his travels was of interest to him. On his return to Europe, he spent 20 years writing down all that he had seen and learned.

▲ Humboldt was a bold adventurer, but also a dedicated scientist who recorded what he had seen.

⊕ HUMIDITY

Humidity is the amount of *water vapor* (water in the form of gas) there is in the air. Have you ever felt sticky and uncomfortable? This may happen when the humidity is high—when there is a lot of water vapor in the air, and the temperature is high.

People say that the humidity is low

▼ When a mass of air is warmed by the sun, it can hold more water vapor. As surface water evaporates, the water vapor is absorbed by the air and its humidity increases. Eventually the air cannot absorb any more water vapor. Evaporation ceases at this point.

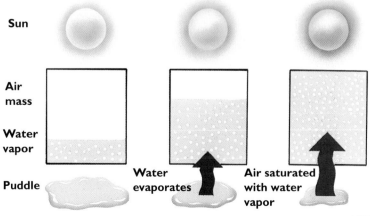

Sun

Air mass

Water vapor

Puddle

Water evaporates

Air saturated with water vapor

when the air contains little water vapor. When the air is very moist, the humidity is high. And when the air holds as much moisture as possible, it is *saturated*. When saturated air cools, it cannot hold as much moisture. Some of the water vapor in the air *condenses*, or changes from gas to tiny droplets of water. Depending on the temperature, these droplets may form fog or clouds, and rain or snow may fall.

The weather report gives a percent number called *relative humidity*. This is the amount of water vapor in the air compared to the amount at which the air would be saturated. For example, if the relative humidity is 99 percent, the air is almost completely saturated with water. Seventy-five degrees Fahrenheit can be very comfortable—if there is a breeze and if the relative humidity is low. But if the air is still, the sky is cloudy, and the relative humidity is high, you may be uncomfortable, even in a tank top. When the humidity is high, perspiration cannot *evaporate* (be taken into the air as a vapor, or gas). The perspiration stays on your skin and you feel sticky. The relative humidity can even help you guess whether it will rain or snow. If the relative humidity is very high in the evening, when the temperature is dropping, you can guess that condensation will occur and it may rain.

▶▶▶▶ **FIND OUT MORE** ◀◀◀◀
Cloud; Fog; Gas; Hail; Rain and Snow; Weather

HUMMINGBIRD

The hummingbird is known for its small size. None of the 400 *species* (kinds) of hummingbirds is large. The largest is the giant hummingbird, which grows to $8\frac{1}{2}$ inches (21 cm) long and lives in the Andes Mountains. Most hummingbirds are about $3\frac{1}{2}$ inches (9 cm) long. But the Cuban bee hummingbird is just over 2 inches (5 cm) long and weighs less than a dime! It is the smallest of all birds.

A hummingbird has a long, slender bill and an even longer tongue. It uses them to reach into flowers and sip the nectar or to gobble up tiny insects and spiders. Hummingbirds help to pollinate many kinds of flowers.

LEARN BY DOING

Scientists calculate relative humidity with a hygrometer. You can make one yourself. You will need two outdoor thermometers that are exactly alike, a brick, some adhesive tape, an old towel, and a pan. Tape the thermometers to the brick. Cut a narrow strip about 8 inches (20 cm) long from the towel. Wrap one end of the strip around the bulb of one of the thermometers and tie in place. Now fill the pan with water and put the other end of the towel strip in it. Soon the whole strip will be wet.

Put your hygrometer in the shade and fan it with paper. The fanning causes water to evaporate from the towel, and the evaporation cools that thermometer. Subtract the wet-bulb temperature from the dry-bulb temperature. Use the chart to find out what the relative humidity is. For example, if the dry-bulb reads 80°F and the wet-bulb reads 79°F, there is a difference of only 1°F. Run your finger across from "1" on the chart, and your other finger down from "80" at the top. What is the percentage of humidity?

CHART FOR FINDING RELATIVE HUMIDITY

Dry-bulb Temperature

	30	40	50	60	70	80	90
0	100%	100%	100%	100%	100%	100%	100%
1	80%	90%	90%	90%	90%	90%	90%
2	70%	80%	80%	80%	90%	90%	90%
3	60%	70%	80%	80%	80%	80%	80%
4	50%	60%	70%	80%	80%	80%	80%
5	40%	60%	60%	70%	70%	70%	80%
6	30%	50%	60%	60%	70%	70%	70%
7	20%	40%	50%	60%	60%	70%	70%
8	10%	30%	40%	50%	60%	60%	70%
9	5%	20%	40%	50%	50%	60%	60%
10	0%	20%	30%	40%	50%	60%	60%

Hummingbirds are also well equipped to reach flowers or to catch insects in flight. They not only can fly forward, they can also fly straight up, sideways or backward. While eating from a flower, they can *hover* (hang in the air). Unlike other birds that flap their wings straight up and down, hummingbirds move their wings in a "figure-eight" motion. Hummingbirds have small, weak feet. They cannot walk or stand on a flat surface, but they can perch on twigs or flower stems.

Hummingbirds come in many shiny colors. The males usually combine two or more colors. Not all females are so colorful.

Hummingbirds live in areas ranging from southern Canada and Alaska to the southern tip of South America. Nineteen kinds are found in the United States. Only one kind, the ruby-throated hummingbird, lives east of the Mississippi River. Its upper feathers are metallic green, its undersides are white and gray, and the male has a ruby red throat. The female lays two eggs in a nest 1½ inches (4 cm) in diameter.

▶ ▶ ▶ ▶ **FIND OUT MORE** ◀ ◀ ◀ ◀
Bird; Flower

HUNDRED YEARS' WAR

A succession of bitter wars, called the Hundred Years' War, was fought between England and France from 1337 to 1453.

The war was started by the English king, Edward III. Edward was the grandson of a former king of France. In 1338, he claimed that he was rightful heir to the crown of France. Relations between the two

▼ The tiny hummingbird has a specially developed beak and tongue that enable it to reach deep inside flowers to feed on nectar and tiny insects.

countries were already tense. Edward held Aquitaine, a large province in southwest France. The French king, Philip VI, was jealous of Edward's power in that region. The French were threatening to limit English trade with Flanders, a province of northern France at that time. Worried English merchants encouraged Edward to take over as king of France.

Some tiny hummingbirds spend 20 hours in the air and make journeys of up to 500 miles (800 km) over water.

▼ At the battle of Crécy in 1346, an English army of 10,000 men defeated a French force of 20,000. Their longbow was faster than the French crossbow.

► Joan of Arc kneeling before the King of France. She is shown in the armor she wore throughout the whole of her campaign.

▲ Edward, Prince of Wales, got his nickname "the Black Prince" from the dark color of his armor.

Magyar, the language of Hungary, is one of the most difficult languages for foreigners to learn. Because of this, little that has been written in Hungarian has been translated into other languages. Even Hungary's best writers are almost unknown to the rest of the world.

► Joan of Arc kneeling before the King of France. She is shown in the armor she wore throughout the whole of her campaign.

Edward landed an army in France in 1346. His troops were mainly foot soldiers, including archers armed with longbows and arrows. The English archers completely routed the best of the French cavalry at the battles of Crécy in 1346 and Edward's son, the Black Prince, did the same at the battle of Poitiers in 1356. The English also captured the important town of Calais. A treaty was signed in 1360. Edward kept Aquitaine and Calais but gave up his claim to the French crown. The war started again in 1369, when the French recaptured Aquitaine.

In the early 1400s, France was torn by civil war. The king was sick and unable to govern. King Henry V of England, seeing the weakness of France, decided to try again for the French crown. Like his ancestor, Edward III, he landed in France with an army. At the Battle of Agincourt in 1415, the English bowmen again caused terrible bloodshed among the French cavalry. Henry signed a treaty with the French in 1422. He married the French king's daughter and was named heir to the French throne. But the two kings both died, within a few months of each other. The French refused to accept Henry's son as their king, and the war broke out again.

The French army was led by a young peasant girl, Joan of Arc. Joan was captured by the English and burned as a witch. But she had given new hope and spirit to the French. By 1453, the English had been driven from all their land in France, except Calais. The war was at an end.

► ► ► ► **FIND OUT MORE** ◄ ◄ ◄ ◄
Edward, Kings of England; French History; Henry, Kings of England; Joan of Arc

HUNGARY

Most of Hungary lies in the Danube River plain in central Europe. It is a *landlocked* country (has no sea-coast), and is surrounded by Austria, the Czech Republic, Slovakia, the Ukraine, Romania, Slovenia, Croatia, and Serbia.

Hungary is mostly a flat country. Mountains partly encircle it. The Austrian Alps lie to the west, and the Carpathian Mountains lie to the north and east. The Danube River flows southward through the center of the nation, toward the Black Sea. Budapest, the capital and largest city, has a port on the river.

Hungary has a humid, *continental*

climate—one unaffected by oceans. Winters are cold, and summers are warm. The climate helps make agriculture the most important part of the economy. Much of the land under cultivation is used for growing corn, wheat, barley, rye, oats, potatoes, and sugar beets. Many fruits are also grown.

Approximately one-third of the Hungarian people work in agriculture. Others work in mining and industry. The chief natural resources developed in Hungary are crude oil, bauxite (the ore from which aluminum is made), brown coal, manganese, and uranium. Sugar beets are refined into sugar, and cloth is woven in textile mills. Machine tools, chemicals, and steel are produced in Hungary, too.

The Hungarian people call themselves Magyars. Their ancestors were an Asian tribe that came to the Danube River plain in the late 800s. Their language, Magyar, is still spoken today. The Hungarians enjoy music and poetry, and the foods they cook are usually spicy. Hungarian folk songs and dances, as well as native dishes such as goulash, are world

famous. Béla Bartók, a Hungarian musician, was one of the world's leading composers in the 1900s.

Through the centuries, the Magyars fiercely defended their land against German, Mongolian, Turkish, and Austrian invaders. Their land became part of the Austrian Empire in 1600. Lajos Kossuth, a Hungarian patriot and statesman, fought for the country's independence from that empire during the 1800s. He was not successful, but many Hungarians today remember him as one of their greatest national heroes.

After World War II, the Soviets invaded Hungary and made it a Communist country. The Hungarians revolted against the Communist rule in 1956, but Soviet troops crushed the uprising with much bloodshed. Many Hungarians fled the country. In 1989, like people of other East European countries, Hungarians voted to abandon Communism. On the 33rd anniversary of the 1956 uprising, they proclaimed a new republic.

HUNGARY

Capital city
Budapest
(2,115,000 people)

Area
35,919 square miles
(93,030 sq. km)

Population
10,563,000 people

Government
Republic

Natural resources
Bauxite, coal, natural gas, oil, manganese, uranium

Export products
Transportation equipment, electrical goods, aluminum, food, wine

Unit of money
Forint

Official language
Hungarian (Magyar)

Salgotarjan • Bukk Mts. • Miskolc • Nyiregyhaza
Ipoly R.
Matra Mts. • Kekes 3,330 ft. 1,015 m. • Eger
Danube R.
Sopron • Gyor • Tatabanya
LITTLE ALFORD
Raba R.
Szombathely • Bakony Mts. • Veszprem
Zala R. • Zalaegerszeg • Sio R. • L. Balaton
Nagykanizsa • Kaposvar • Szekszard
Mecsek Mts. • Pecs
Drava R.
Szekesfehervar • Szolnok
Dunaujvaros • Kecskemet
Hodmezovasarhely • Szeged • Maros R.
Tisza R.
Kiskorei Res.
Debrecen
ALFORD
Koros R.
Kiskorei Res.
GREAT
Bekescsaba
Budapest

N W E S

0 50 100 Miles
0 50 100 150 Kilometers
© 1994 GeoSystems, an R.R. Donnelley & Sons Company

▼ **A view of Buda and Pest, the two halves of Hungary's capital, Budapest. The Danube River divides them.**

▲ A photograph of hurricane Hugo taken by a weather satellite. Satellites are very helpful in giving warnings of bad weather to come.

▼ In a typical hurricane, the winds rise as high as the troposphere (up to 10 miles above the Earth's surface) before losing their force.

HURRICANE

A hurricane is a powerful tropical storm. To be called a hurricane, a storm must have wind speeds of at least 74 miles per hour (117 km/h).

People who live around the eastern and western Pacific Ocean call hurricanes *typhoons*. People who live on the Indian Ocean call them *cyclones*. Whatever name is used, a hurricane is a terrible windstorm that includes heavy rains, high waves, and high tides. Hurricane winds whirl around in a great circle. In a severe storm, the winds may reach speeds of 200 miles an hour (322 km/hr).

Hurricanes form over tropical oceans not far from the equator, where the air is very moist. Certain weather conditions, such as a thunderstorm, may cause great quantities of moisture to *condense* (turn from vapor to droplets of water). The condensing moisture gives off large amounts of heat, which warms the air. The warmed air rises, and as the Earth rotates, the column of warm air begins to spin. This is the beginning of a hurricane. Hurricanes occur in the North Atlantic Ocean from June to November when the sea sur-

face is warmest and the air humidity highest. In the Northern Hemisphere, a hurricane spins counterclockwise; in the Southern Hemisphere, it spins clockwise.

The whirling mass of air spreads for several days. The largest hurricanes have measured nearly 1,000 miles (1,600 km) across. At this stage, the air begins to move forward at speeds of about 10 miles an hour (16 km/hr). But after the storm turns away from the equator, its speed increases to 30 or 40 miles an hour (48 to 64 km/hr). As the storm moves, the moisture falls as torrents of rain. At the center of the hurricane is a narrow column of air that spins very slowly. This is the *eye* of the hurricane.

A hurricane becomes weaker as it moves over land because it needs the warm sea to supply energy by evaporation. Friction between the land and wind also uses up the storm's energy.

▶▶▶▶ **FIND OUT MORE** ◀◀◀◀
Cloud; Humidity; Lightning and Thunder

HUXLEY FAMILY

Four members of the famous Huxley family have made valuable contributions to both science and literature.

Thomas Henry Huxley (1825–1895) wrote and lectured in favor of Darwin's theory of evolution. Huxley graduated from medical school and spent four years exploring the South Pacific. His observations of jellyfish led to important evidence about the theory of evolution.

Sir Julian Sorell Huxley (1887–1975) was Director General of the United Nations Educational, Scientific, and Cultural Organization (UNESCO). Like his grandfather, he was interested in evolution. Huxley made studies of birds. He discovered that some parts of an animal grow faster than other parts.

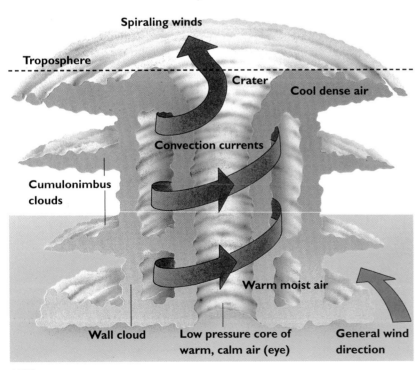

Spiraling winds

Troposphere

Crater

Cool dense air

Convection currents

Cumulonimbus clouds

Warm moist air

Wall cloud

Low pressure core of warm, calm air (eye)

General wind direction

Aldous Leonard Huxley (1894–1963) was a famous writer. In *Point Counter Point* (1928), he *satirizes* (points out the foolishness of something by making fun of it) the failings of modern civilization. *Brave New World* (1932) is Huxley's vision of what will happen to human life in the future. He felt that people were developing a society in which machines and science mattered more than people. Huxley revealed in his novels his interest in religion, in the way the mind works, and in the effect of science on people.

Andrew Fielding Huxley (1917–), the half brother of Julian and Aldous, is a biologist who shared the 1963 Nobel prize in physiology and medicine with two other scientists. They were awarded the prize for their work on nerve impulses.

▶ ▶ ▶ **FIND OUT MORE** ◀ ◀ ◀
Darwin, Charles; Evolution; Literature

HYDRA

A hydra is a small brown or green animal with a big appetite. It is a freshwater relative of the sea anemone. Its tiny, soft, tubular body is usually anchored to a water plant.

▼ **The hydra lives in ponds and streams, attaching itself to water plants and feeding on small life forms.**

Several *tentacles*, or arms, wave around the hydra's mouth. The arms are covered with miniature lassos and stinging harpoons that whip out to capture water fleas, tiny fish, tadpoles and any other small animals that bump into the hydra. The prey is often larger than the hydra itself, but its elastic-sided body can accommodate the meal.

Branches often grow from the hydra's body and produce their own tentacles for catching food. The branches eventually break away and start life as separate creatures.

⚙ HYDRAULICS

The brakes of a car need a lot of power to bring the car to a halt. The driver's foot pushes the brake pedal. Then a system of hydraulics connects the pedal to the brakes. The hydraulic system magnifies the small force of the driver's foot and operates the brakes with great power.

The hydraulic system in a car contains a set of cylinders connected together by pipes containing a special liquid called hydraulic fluid. Inside each cylinder, a piston can move up and down. One cylinder, the master cylinder, is connected to the brake pedal. The other cylinders, the slave cylinders, are inside the brakes.

When the brake pedal is pressed, it pushes the piston down in the master cylinder. This action increases the pressure of the fluid inside the pipes and slave cylinders. The fluid then forces up the pistons in the slave cylinders with great strength, and the pistons operate the brakes.

Hydraulic systems are fitted in excavators, cranes, and presses that stamp large sheets of metal into shape. Hydraulics are also used to power robots.

◀ **Thomas Huxley, English biologist, who supported Darwin's theories.**

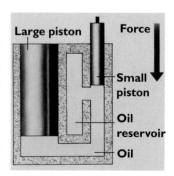

▲ **Aldous Huxley, famous for his book *Brave New World*, which made many people think about society.**

▼ **Hydraulics at work in a hydraulic jack. A large movement of the small piston causes a smaller movement of the larger piston. But the larger piston acts with a much greater force than the smaller one.**

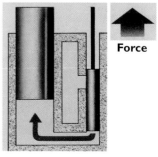

Large piston   Force
Small piston
Oil reservoir
Oil

Force

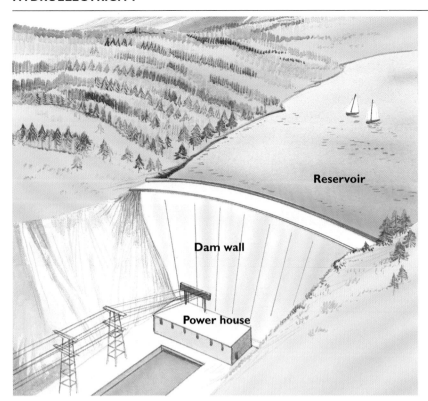

▲ **Hydroelectric power stations use the power of moving water to produce electricity. Most stations store water in a reservoir behind a dam wall. The water drives turbines to produce electricity.**

The giant Hoover Dam on the Colorado River supplies hydroelectric power to Southern California, Arizona, and Nevada. Building the dam meant flooding 247 square miles (640 sq. km) of the land, creating Lake Mead. The water from the dam pours down through a giant steel pipe 30 feet (9 m) in diameter. It then branches out into 16 smaller pipes, each 13 feet (4 m) wide, which lead to the turbines. The generators produce nearly 1.5 million kilowatts of electric power. (An electric toaster uses about one kilowatt.)

⚙ HYDROELECTRICITY

More than one-fifth of all the world's electricity is produced by using the energy of fast-moving water. We call electricity *generated* (made) in this way *hydroelectricity*, or *hydroelectric power*.

Everything moving has *kinetic energy*, (energy because of its motion). Moving water has kinetic energy, and it is possible to make that kinetic energy into electric energy using machines called *turbines* and *generators*. A turbine is like a big wheel. When water falls on the turbine, the wheel spins. This works a generator to make electricity.

Most hydroelectric plants are built into dams, although some smaller ones are in waterfalls.

The most efficient way of using hydroelectricity is the *pumped-storage system*. At different times of day (mealtimes, for example), people want more electricity (for cooking). When people are using less electricity (in the middle of the night), water is pumped into a special reservoir. This stored water can be used to generate extra electricity at busy times of day.

Tidal power makes use of big changes in water depths caused by the ocean tides. At high tide, water flowing into a river mouth is used to fill a high reservoir. At low tide, this water pours out and passes through turbines to generate electricity.

▶▶▶▶ **FIND OUT MORE** ◀◀◀◀
Dam; Electricity; Electric Power; Electromagnet; Engine

⚙ HYDROFOIL

A trip in a fast motorboat is fun. The boat speeds over the water so fast it almost seems ready to take off and fly. A boat called a *hydrofoil* gets even closer to leaving the water. Underneath the hull of a hydrofoil are winglike structures. As the hydrofoil travels faster, these wings produce lift (just like an airplane's wings) and force the hydrofoil boat upward.

When racing at full speed, a hydrofoil skims along on its wings. With most of its hull clear of the water, it is not held back by the water's resistance. It can also turn and come to a stop very quickly.

The first hydrofoil boat was built in Italy about 1900. Today, they are used as ferries, pleasure boats, and also by the U.S. Navy. They can reach speeds of more than 70 miles per hour (112 km/h).

▶▶▶▶ **FIND OUT MORE** ◀◀◀◀
Boats and Boating

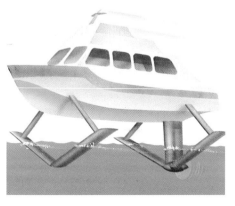

▲ **Hydrofoils usually give sea travelers a smoother and faster journey.**

⚙ HYDROGEN

Although hydrogen is the most abundant chemical element in the universe, it forms only one percent of the Earth's crust and atmosphere. Hydrogen is abundant in the sun and other stars. Much of the heat given off by the sun is caused by the fusion of hydrogen atoms to form helium.

Free hydrogen—a colorless, tasteless, odorless gas—is found only in very small amounts in the Earth and its atmosphere. But hydrogen combines very easily with other elements, and is widely distributed over the Earth. The most important and abundant hydrogen compound is water, H_2O, which is made up of two atoms of hydrogen for every one atom of oxygen. Hydrogen and carbon combine in various ways to form *hydrocarbons*, such as petroleum products, coal products, and rubber. Hydrogen, combined with other substances, is found in all plant and animal cells. Much of the food we eat is in the form of carbohydrates, compounds of hydrogen, oxygen and carbon. Sugar and starches are carbohydrates. All acids contain hydrogen. Hydrochloric acid is present in the stomach. It aids digestion of food.

Hydrogen, with its many compounds, is a very useful element. Hydrogen peroxide, H_2O_2, is used as an antiseptic and a bleaching agent. Enormous amounts of hydrogen are used in the manufacture of ammonia (fertilizers, disinfectants) and methyl alcohol (antifreeze, fuel).

Hydrogen is so light it was once used to inflate balloons and airships (blimps). But hydrogen is highly *combustible*—when mixed with air or oxygen and *ignited* (set on fire), it explodes. So helium gas has replaced hydrogen in balloons and airships.

▶ ▶ ▶ ▶ **FIND OUT MORE** ◀ ◀ ◀ ◀
Atom; Balloon; Carbohydrate;
Cell; Chemistry; Element; Gas;
Gasoline; Water

▨ HYENA

Hyenas are *carnivorous* (meat-eating) mammals. They often roam in packs, hunting and killing zebras, antelopes, cattle, and other animals. Because hyenas also feed on *carrion* (the remains of dead animals) and garbage, they are useful as scavengers.

Some hyenas can grow to over 5 feet (1.5 m) in length and can weigh over 200 pounds (90 kg). The forelegs of hyenas are longer than their hind legs. Each foot has four claw-tipped toes. Their heads are large with long, pointed ears. Their jaws, jaw muscles, and teeth are strong enough to crush thick bones.

There are three main kinds of hyenas. The *spotted*, or *laughing*, hyena is the largest kind. It has yellowish-gray hair with black spots and is found in Africa, south of the Sahara. The *brown hyena* of South Africa has long dark brown hair. The *striped hyena* is grayish-brown with dark stripes and lives in North Africa, India, and the Near East.

The *aardwolf* ("earth wolf") of southern Africa is a close relative of the hyena, but lives a very different kind of life. Like the hyena, it hunts for food at night, almost always alone. The aardwolf is only about 30 inches (75 cm) long, including its tail. Unlike real hyenas, the aardwolf has small teeth and a weak jaw. Termites and other insects are its main food. It may sometimes eat dead flesh.

▶ ▶ ▶ ▶ **FIND OUT MORE** ◀ ◀ ◀ ◀
Carnivore; Mammal

HYGROMETER

SEE HUMIDITY

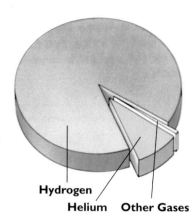

Hydrogen
Helium   Other Gases

▲ **This pie chart shows the proportions of the gases that make up our sun. Hydrogen is the main component by far. It is found in a great many compounds.**

Hydrogen is 14.4 times lighter than air and is the lightest substance known.

▲ **The hyena is often thought to be cowardly. But in fact, a group of hyenas will drive a lion from its kill.**

☼ HYPNOTISM

The term *hypnosis* comes from the Greek word *hypnos* meaning "sleep." However, hypnosis does not put people to sleep. Instead it puts them into a warm state of relaxation.

"Look at that spot on the ceiling... Your eyes are becoming heavy... When I count to three, you will not be able to raise your right hand." How many times have you heard words like these on television or in motion pictures?

The person looking at the ceiling is taking part in a demonstration of *hypnotism*. The person giving the commands is a *hypnotist*. A hypnotized person is in a temporary state, called "hypnosis," during which his or her attention is changed and often concentrated.

There are many mistaken ideas about how hypnotism is induced, and what it can achieve. The most important thing to remember is that the willingness to become hypnotized comes from within a person, and involves no magic or outside forces.

Hypnotism does not put someone to sleep. Instead it is a way of getting the person to concentrate on certain things without being distracted by anything else. During hypnosis a person becomes open to the hypnotist's suggestions, and can become hungry, blind, or hot. Some people can imagine that they are five years old again.

Clues uncovered during hypnosis can help treat many illnesses. The cause of a present illness or *phobia* (irrational fear of something) might be a forgotten childhood incident, such as being bitten by a dog.

The scientific study of hypnotism is about 100 years old, although there are descriptions of similar trances in the writings of many ancient cultures. An Austrian doctor, Franz Anton Mesmer, used magnetic wands to treat sick people in the 1770s. He thought that there were invisible magnetic fluids in the human body. Although the people claimed to be cured, scientists could find no evidence of magnetic fluids. They concluded that the patients had really been cured by Dr. Mesmer's powerful suggestions.

Discoveries by a British doctor, James Braid, and a French scientist, Jean Martin Charcot, led to the development of hypnotism as a branch of science during the 1800s. In the early 1900s, Sigmund Freud, the famous Austrian psychiatrist, used hypnotism to get patients to recall incidents that had occurred many years before.

At the same time there were people who tried to turn hypnotism into public entertainment. Many people began to think of hypnotism as a circus sideshow, with little real value.

Gradually hypnotism regained respectability. New laws prevented unqualified people from hypnotizing others. The medical profession provided clear guidelines on how hypnotism should be used by doctors, dentists, and other medical personnel.

Hypnotism continues to be used as a treatment for physical and mental illness. It has also been used to help witnesses of crime to present evidence. And controlled hypnosis has proved effective in helping people control their eating, drinking, smoking, and sleeping.

▶ ▶ ▶ ▶ **FIND OUT MORE** ◀ ◀ ◀ ◀
Freud, Sigmund;
Psychology and Psychiatry

▼ A hypnotherapist attempts to treat many problems using hypnosis, especially behavioral problems such as smoking and bad eating habits. In a state of extreme relaxation the patient is able to respond to suggestions made by the hypnotherapist.

IBN BATUTA (1304–1368)

One of the greatest travelers of the Middle Ages was an Arab scholar, Ibn Batuta (also spelled Battuta). He wrote a famous book about his journeys.

Ibn Batuta was born in Morocco, North Africa. He set out at age 21 to make a pilgrimage to Mecca, as a religious duty. The sight of foreign countries, with new customs and new ideas, fired his imagination. For more than 25 years he was received with honor by princes, sultans, and other rulers. He visited Constantinople, Samarkand, India, China, Sumatra, Moorish Spain, and even crossed the Sahara Desert to the empire of Mali.

Traveling mostly on foot, on horseback or by boat, Ibn Batuta traveled the amazing distance of 75,000 miles (121,000 km).

Ibn Batuta.

IBSEN, HENRIK (1828–1906)

Ibsen was Norway's greatest playwright. He is often called the first modern playwright. He wrote about the problems of society and of individual men and women. His plays shocked the audiences of his day. People were not used to watching "psychological" dramas about serious real-life problems.

Henrik Ibsen was born in Skien, Norway. He began to write as a young boy. He studied medicine, but gave it up to become a *dramatist* (writer of plays). Ibsen was

▶ **Henrik Ibsen, the famous Norwegian playwright.**

also a stage manager and director of theaters in Christiania (now Oslo). He was awarded a travel scholarship and a writer's allowance by the Norwegian government and spent many years in Germany.

One of Ibsen's most famous plays is *A Doll's House*, about a woman who leaves a troubled marriage to lead an independent life. Another is *Hedda Gabler*, a dark and tragic story of an unhappy woman who kills herself. In his play, An *Enemy of the People*, Ibsen presented a problem that still confronts us today—pollution. Ibsen believed in the rights of women and in people being responsible for their environment. His timeless writing has had an enormous effect on drama throughout the world.

▶ ▶ ▶ ▶ **FIND OUT MORE** ◀ ◀ ◀ ◀
Drama

ICE AGE

At least five times during the Earth's history, huge ice sheets have slowly moved from the north and south polar regions toward the equator, and covered much of the northern and southern halves of our planet. These periods, each lasting millions of years, were ice ages.

It is wrong to think that the climate is very cold all through an ice age. Each ice age has had a number of *glacials* (very cold periods), but between these have been *interglacials* (warmer periods).

DEVELOPMENT OF THE LETTER I

The Egyptian I
c. 3000 B.C.

The Phoenician I
c. 1000 B.C.

The Greek I
c. 600 B.C.

The Roman I
c. A.D. 600

▶ During the last Ice Age, the ice cap at the North Pole was much larger than today. It covered most of Europe and North America.

At the peak of the last ice age almost a third of the Earth was covered with ice. Only about 10 percent of the Earth is ice-covered today.

If all the ice on Earth melted at the same time, the world's oceans would rise by about 180 feet (55 m). New York's skyscrapers would be in water as high as the eighteenth floor.

▼ During past Ice Ages, woolly mammoths roamed the plains of Europe and North America. They looked rather like large, shaggy-haired elephants.

During an interglacial, the climate may even be warmer than it is normally. Many scientists believe we are living now in an interglacial, and that the next glacial will begin in a few thousand years' time.

The last glacial ended about 10,000 years ago. In North America, the glaciers covered all of Canada and northern parts of the United States.

These vast glaciers (*ice sheets* or *continental glaciers*) made big changes to the Earth's surface as they scraped over it. The Great Lakes were probably gouged out by the glaciers of the last glacial. The fiords of Norway, Alaska, Greenland, Chile, and New Zealand are valleys carved out by the moving glaciers, and now flooded by the sea.

The most recent (or current) ice age lasted about 10 million years. Most ice ages have lasted much longer than this, which is why scientists believe that this ice age is not yet over. This ice age is called the *Pleistocene Ice Age*. Earlier ones started about 300 million years ago, about 450 million years ago, about 600 million years ago, and about 750 million years ago.

There may also have been others. During the most recent ice age, mammals that had adapted to life in a cold climate roamed the Earth. Among them were woolly mammoths, woolly rhinoceroses, and giant wolves. Prehistoric people also lived through this ice age.

No one knows exactly what causes ice ages. Some scientists think that the amount of heat given out by the sun changes from time to time. Others have noticed that ice ages seem to happen once every 150 million years or so. As our solar system goes in its orbit around the center of our galaxy, it passes, roughly every 150 million years, through regions of space containing more dust and gas than is usual. Scientists argue as to why this might cause an ice age. Another theory is that ice ages start when large continents drift into polar regions. Antarctica is in such a position today.

Astronomers believe that the planet Mars is currently suffering an ice age.

▶▶▶▶ **FIND OUT MORE** ◀◀◀◀
Continental Drift; Earth History; Glacier; Mammals of the Past; Solar System; Milky Way

ICEBERG

If a glacier reaches the sea, its forward edge breaks off, forming huge floating blocks of ice called *icebergs*.

If the glacier reaches the sea over a cliff, ice breaks off and falls into the water. Icebergs formed this way are of moderate size. A glacier also may enter the ocean below sea level. Because its ice is lighter than water, it will be forced upward until it breaks off, forming very large icebergs. The process of forming icebergs is called *calving*. Icebergs are made up of

freshwater ice, since they are formed on land from snowfalls.

In the North Atlantic Ocean, the main sources of icebergs are the glaciers of Greenland. The average height of a Greenland iceberg is 800 feet (240 m). Only 100 feet (30 m) rises above the surface of the ocean, and the remaining seven-eighths of the iceberg is below the surface. In Antarctic waters, icebergs rising more than 500 feet (150 m) above the surface of the ocean have been reported. This means that about 3,500 feet (roughly 1,050 m) are below the surface. Icebergs drift into warmer water where they melt and finally disappear.

Icebergs do not come from the ice that forms the frozen surface of the Arctic and Antarctic oceans. This ice is only a few feet thick, and breaks off in broad sheets.

In 1912, the large ocean liner *Titanic* struck an iceberg in the North Atlantic Ocean, and sank. Many passengers and crew members lost their lives. Following this disaster, the United States Coast Guard established an iceberg patrol in the North Atlantic shipping lanes. The patrol seeks out icebergs, and warns ships of their location.

▶▶▶▶ **FIND OUT MORE** ◀◀◀◀
Glacier

ICE CREAM

Ice cream is a frozen dairy food, popular in many countries of the world. It is mostly a mixture of milk products, sugar, and water. Sometimes egg whites, gelatin, cocoa, fruits, or nuts are added. Because ice cream has many fats and carbohydrates, it is high in calories.

Standard ice cream contains at least 20 percent milk fat and other milk solids. Ice milk has less—at least 11 percent—and sherbet has only two percent. Some frozen products contain vegetable oils instead of milk fat.

Commercial Ice Cream

Federal and state laws regulate production of ice cream in factories. They limit the amount of air whipped into the product, and require that certain ingredients must be included in certain proportions in order to call a product "ice cream."

Large manufacturers use a continuous process, pushing the mixture through pipes. They start with fresh pasteurized milk solids, add water and sugar and sometimes other ingredients, and *homogenize* it, or break up the particles of fat. This makes a smoother ice cream. This mix is cooled in cold pipes to about

▲ Huge icebergs float because *ice* (frozen water that has expanded) is less *dense* (heavy) than water.

▼ Ice cream is one of the world's most popular foods. It can be served in cones, sundaes, dishes, sodas, and many other ways. This is an ice cream sundae.

LEARN BY DOING

You can make ice cream in the ice-cube trays of your refrigerator. To do this mix together: one can of sweetened condensed milk, two cups of fresh whole milk, and two teaspoons of lemon juice. Freeze the mixture in the trays until it is mushy. Put it into a cold bowl and beat it with a cold egg beater or spoon. Mix in two teaspoons of vanilla extract (or instead, you can add cut-up fruit). Refreeze the mixture in the trays until it is solid.

35° F (1.5°C). This keeps germs from growing in it. It goes through pipes to big stirring tanks, then to flavoring tanks. Finally the mushy mixture is piped into a freezing tube, where it freezes soft—about 32°F (O°C). It is then molded into bars, put into sandwiches, or piped into cartons that are closed by machine. Then it is frozen solid and shipped to sellers.

Ice cream was once a luxury food that most people rarely had a chance to enjoy. After the beginning of the manufacture of commercial ice cream in the United States in 1851, ice cream became a favorite food. Ice-cream parlors offer a variety of flavors and colors to tempt almost anyone. And additional nuts and fresh fruit make it a very special dessert. Plus, today, it is easily kept frozen in people's own home freezers.

▶ ▶ ▶ ▶ **FIND OUT MORE** ◀ ◀ ◀ ◀
Dairy Products

ICE HOCKEY

Many sports fans consider ice hockey to be one of the most exciting sports. The game is played on ice by players who wear ice skates. Because it is a game that began in cold climates, ice hockey is most popular in cold regions, especially in Canada. The game is played in some high schools and colleges, as well as by professional hockey players. Several cities in the United States and Canada have professional ice hockey teams belonging to the National Hockey League (NHL). This is ice hockey's major professional league. Teams compete for the championship Stanley Cup each year.

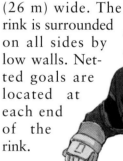

Professional ice hockey is played in a *rink* (playing area) that is usually 200 feet (61 m) long and 85 feet (26 m) wide. The rink is surrounded on all sides by low walls. Netted goals are located at each end of the rink.

An ice hockey team consists of six players— three forwards, two defensemen, and the goalkeeper, or goalie. They use wooden hockey sticks that have a long handle and a curved blade at the bottom. The stick is used to move the *puck*. The puck is a round rubber disk weighing between 5½ and 6 ounces (155–170 grams). The object of the game is to score goals by shooting the puck past the goalie of the opposing team and into the net of the goal.

Ice hockey is not only a very fast

▼ **The playing area of an ice hockey rink. The rink is divided into three zones.**

▶ **Ice hockey players wear padding under their clothes for protection.**

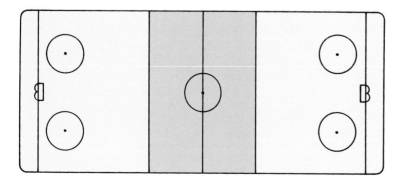

game, but it is also a rough one. The players wear helmets and heavily padded gloves, as well as pads on their shoulders and legs. The goalie wears large leg pads and sometimes a protective face mask. The goalie's hockey stick is extra wide to help stop the puck when the opponents shoot it at the goal.

ICELAND

The country of Iceland is a mountainous island of volcanic rock, lying in the North Atlantic Ocean, just south of the Arctic Circle. Reykjavik, its capital and largest city, is the northernmost capital in the world. A branch of the warm Gulf Stream flows around the western and southern coasts and part of the northern coast. Most of the people live on the coastal lowlands, where temperatures are mild.

The windswept landscape is bare except for some grass and a few shrubs. Snowcapped mountains rise out of brownish lava fields. About one-eighth of Iceland is covered by huge, thick glaciers. Ancient glaciers have dug holes in the land, forming lakes, and have cut deep *fiords* (long, narrow inlets) along the coast, creating natural harbors. Millions of ducks, geese, gulls, and other birds nest near lakes, rivers, and on coastal cliffs. Trout and salmon are common in lakes and rivers. No wild animals live on the island except for a few fox, reindeer, and rodents. Seals and whales are found along the coast.

Some of Iceland's volcanoes are active. Fire that burns inside the Earth heats rainwater trickling through rocks. Steam and boiling water spout from the Earth as hot springs and geysers. Hot water is piped from springs to heat Reykjavik and other towns. Reykjavik is called a "smokeless city," since steam causes no pollution. The steam helps grow vegetables and fruit, including grapes and bananas, in greenhouses. Warm water pumped from underground fills outdoor swimming pools that are open all year.

Many people earn their living by fishing and processing fish, mainly cod and herring. Farmers grow hay to feed to sheep and horses. Potatoes and turnips are also grown. Major industries include cement making and aluminum smelting.

Most Icelanders are descendants of Norsemen or Vikings who came from Norway in the 800s. People today still speak the old language of their ancestors. Iceland's parliament, called the *Althing*, was formed in A.D. 930, and is now the world's oldest parliament. The island first belonged to Norway and later to Denmark. Iceland became an independent republic in 1944 after breaking its ties with Denmark.

▶▶▶▶ **FIND OUT MORE** ◀◀◀◀
Europe; Fishing Industry; Geyser; Scandinavian Languages; Volcano

ICELAND

Capital city
Reykjavik
(95,800 people)

Area
39,769 square miles
(103,000 sq. km)

Population
255,000 people

Government
Republic

Natural resources
Thermal (steam) and water

Export products
Fish, fish products, animal products, aluminum, diatomite

Unit of money
Krona

Official language
Icelandic

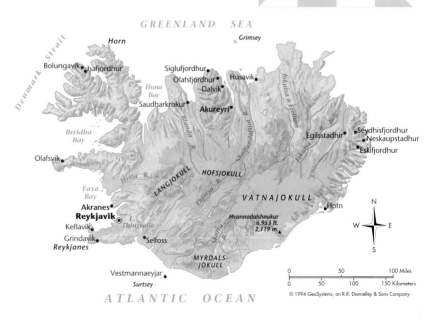

▼ The axel jump, shown here, is named for the Norwegian Axel Paulsen. Skaters in competitions are penalized for landing on both skates.

▼ The long blade of the speed skate contrasts with the blade of the figure skate.

Speed skate

Figure skate

▼ In free-skating competition, single skaters interpret music of their choice by expressive movements.

ICE SKATING

One of the most graceful forms of sport and entertainment is ice skating. Each year there are national championships and world championships. Ice skating is also an important part of the Olympic Games.

At one time, people could ice skate only in regions where the winter was long and cold. In North America, only Canada and the northern United States could offer a chance for months of ice skating. In Europe, ice skating was limited to the Scandinavian countries and other northern nations.

Indoor ice rinks were first developed in the 1930s. These indoor rinks provide ice skating opportunities all year round for people who, in the past, could skate only in the winter, or had no chance to enjoy the sport at all.

Learning to Ice Skate

It is best to learn ice skating when you are young. In most large cities, there is at least one indoor skating rink, where there are skating instructors. There may also be a skating club at the rink.

Most experts agree on this method for beginners taking their first steps on ice skates: The new skaters take chairs on the ice and hold onto the back of them. The chairs give the beginners some support and help them get the feel of skating on ice. After learning the skating stroke, by pushing off with one foot and then the other, the skaters can put away their chairs and be on their own. They may fall a few times—everyone does—but it's not a painful fall.

Ice Skates

The blades of skates used in the various forms of ice skating differ. Figure skates have blades that are rounded in front. The front edges of these skates have little teeth like a saw. Hockey skates are thinner and pointed in front with no saw teeth, and the shoes have hard toes. Racing skates have extra long, thin blades.

The first ice skates were wooden or bone runners, something like tiny skis, that were clamped to the skater's shoes. Later, the skates were made of metal, but were still clamped to shoes. Today, most skates are permanently attached to special skating shoes. The fit of the shoes is the most important thing about skates. The shoes must fit perfectly and they must be laced correctly. The laces need not be tight at the top and bottom, but the laces must be tight in the middle, where the shoe curves around the ankle. Tight laces provide ankle support. Sometimes, ice skates can be bought or rented at the rink.

Figure Skating

Ice hockey is dramatic and speed skating is exciting, but figure skating is considered by many to be the most perfect form of ice skating. Figure skating gets its name from the designs, or figures, that the skates make on the surface of the ice. In a *figure eight*, for example, the skates make ice grooves that resemble the numeral 8.

Figure skating requires the grace of a ballet dancer combined with the coordination of a top athlete. In competitive skating, there are competitions for men and women solo skaters, for pairs, and for ice dancing.

▶ ▶ ▶ ▶ **FIND OUT MORE** ◀ ◀ ◀ ◀
Ice Hockey; Olympic Games; Sports

IDAHO

Shoshone County, in northern Idaho, is grateful to a runaway mule. The mule belonged to a man named Noah Kellogg. Back in 1884, Kellogg was traveling through the Bitterroot Mountains. (These mountains are on the border between Idaho and Montana.) A mule was carrying Kellogg's belongings. One night the mule wandered off. His owner went looking for him the next day. When at last he found the animal, Kellogg spied something shiny among the rocks. The mule had led him to ore! It proved to be lead and silver.

There is a town named Kellogg in Shoshone County today. Near it is the Sunshine Mine. This silver mine is the largest in the United States. A big lead mine is also nearby. Kellogg lies at the heart of northern Idaho's rich mining region.

The Land and Climate
Idaho is in the Rocky Mountains. Two other Rocky Mountain states—Nevada and Utah—are on its southern border. Idaho's neighbors to the west are Washington and Oregon. Montana and Wyoming are to the east. The northern part of Idaho is called the Panhandle. It is narrow compared with the rest of the state. The tip of the Panhandle, bordering on Canada, is only 45 miles (72 km) wide.

Idaho has three very different land regions—the narrow north, the wide south, and middle Idaho. The rugged mountains of middle Idaho separate it from the other two parts.

In general, Idaho is dry. But there are great differences throughout the state. The northern and western areas receive most of the state's *precipitation* (rain and snow). Winter snow is deep in the higher mountains.

Blue lakes and shining rivers make northern Idaho beautiful. The deep Pend Oreille Lake is a favorite spot for fishing in the summer.

Coeur d'Alene Lake is popular with vacationers. Northern Idaho's mining district is scarred by mine waste. But outside this area, the land is very pleasant. Mountains are covered with forests. Valleys are planted with crops. Some of the farmers still live in log houses.

Lewiston is the largest city in northern Idaho, although it has only about 28,000 people. The city is a river port. Boats from the west can reach Lewiston via the Snake River. Around the city are wheat and pea farms, and fruit orchards.

Farther up the Snake River is North America's deepest gorge, Hells Canyon, which is 7,900 feet (2,400 m) deep at one point.

The Clearwater Mountains, which include the rugged granite Bighorn Crags, are in middle Idaho and overlook the Salmon River to the south. The Salmon flows so swiftly that going down it is a real adventure. But no one ever goes up the Salmon. That is why people call it the "River of No Return." The basin of this

▲ The sun glinting on the spectacular Shoshone falls, found in northern Idaho.

▲ An adventurous group risks danger for the thrill of the fast-flowing Salmon River.

1339

IDAHO

Capital and largest city
Boise (125,738 people)

Area
83,557 square miles
(216,412 sq. km)

Population
1,006,749 people
Rank: 42nd

Statehood
July 3, 1890
(43rd state admitted)

Principal river
Snake River

Highest point
Borah Peak: 12,662 feet
(3,859 m)

Motto
Esta Perpetua
("It is forever")

Song
"Here We Have Idaho"

Famous people
Ezra Pound, Gutzon Borglum, William Borah, Sacagawea

STATE SYMBOLS

▲ A sprig of the lovely syringa, adopted March 2, 1931.

▼ The mountain bluebird feeds on insects and fruit.

▲ The images on this seal show that the state's main industries are mining, forestry, and farming.

▶ The western white pine lives for hundreds of years.

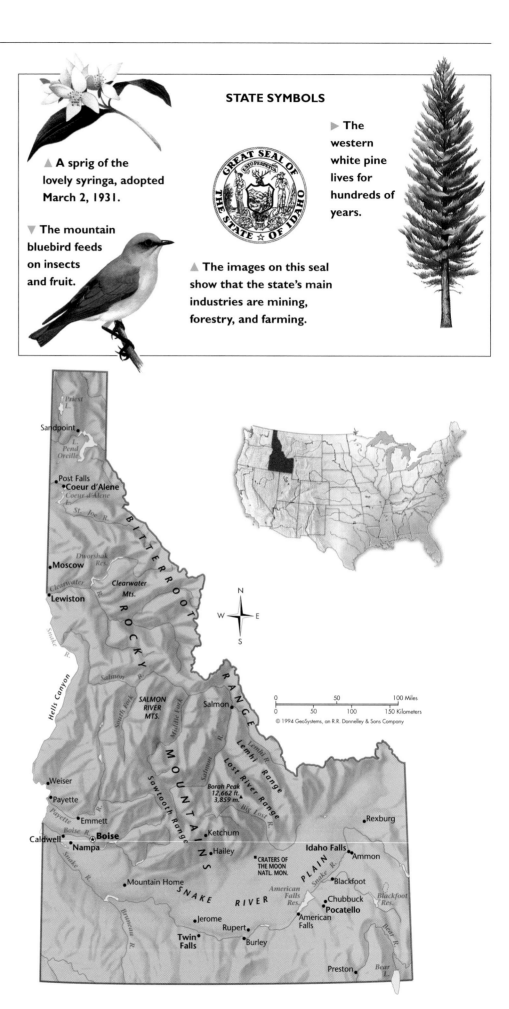

© 1994 GeoSystems, an R.R. Donnelley & Sons Company

river is a wilderness of lakes, mountains, flowery meadows, and untouched forests. The Salmon River Mountains rise to the south of the Salmon River Basin. They are even higher than the Clearwater Mountains. The beautiful Sawtooth Mountains are found farther south.

Southern Idaho is mostly part of the Snake River Basin. The river flows in a great curve through beds of lava. This lava flowed from volcanoes many years ago. Mouths of old volcanoes can be seen at Craters of the Moon National Monument.

The southern part of Idaho is very dry. In some places the wind has piled sand into hills, or dunes. The broad green fields of the Snake River Basin are green only because they are irrigated. This part of Idaho is the state's best farming region. Potatoes, sugar beets, and wheat are its main crops. Cattle and sheep are also raised in the Snake River Basin.

History

Part of Idaho's story can be read in the names of places and tribes.

The Native Americans were the first people living on the land. Our word *Idaho* comes from the Shoshone word *Ee-dah-how*, meaning "It's sunrise." This seems to have been a "good morning" greeting. At the time the first white men arrived, there were five large tribes—three in the north and two in the south. One northern tribe was the *Nez Percé* (French for "Pierced Nose"). These Native Americans pierced their noses for ornaments. The second tribe, the *Pend d'Oreille* (French for "Eardrop"), may have gotten their name because they wore earrings at one time. The third northern tribe was the *Coeur d'Alene* (French for "Heart of Awl"). *Awls* are sharp, pointed tools used to make holes in wood and leather. Perhaps the French fur traders thought the Native Americans were hard and sharp in bargaining. And the Native Americans

might have thought that the traders were. The two main southern tribes were the *Shoshone* (Native American word meaning "Great Spirit") and the *Bannock* (this Native American word was the name of the tuft of hair combed back from the forehead of a warrior).

The first white people in Idaho were French trappers and fur traders, who traded with the Native Americans.

The American explorers Meriwether Lewis and William Clark passed through Idaho in 1805 and 1806. A young Native American woman, Sacagawea, acted as their guide and translator when dealing with the Shoshone tribe. They crossed the area where Lewiston stands today.

Gold was discovered near the Clearwater River in 1860. People came to the area in large numbers. Ranches and farms were started by people who wanted to sell food to the miners. The white settlers took Native American land, and the tribes fought them.

▲ **The sun has set on a modern ranch in the heartland of Idaho.**

▼ **St. Anthony's glorious sand dunes in Idaho offer the perfect setting for sand-buggy racing.**

▶ **The lava-rich soils that spread southward from the Snake River provide fertile growing ground for Idaho's important potato production.**

The first Ferris wheel was erected in Chicago, Illinois, at the Columbian Exposition in 1893. It was made up of 36 cars, and each car held 60 passengers. The highest point of the wheel was 264 feet (80 m). The wheel was named after its inventor, George Washington Gale Ferris.

Noah Kellogg's discovery of silver and lead in 1884 brought more settlers to Idaho. Idaho was made a state six years after the discovery.

Working in Idaho

Agriculture still brings in the most money in Idaho. Crops earn more than livestock, although both are important. Potatoes are the leading crop, followed by wheat, sugar beets, and hay. Beef cattle and sheep are raised.

Manufacturing is a fairly close second to agriculture. Factories are found chiefly in Boise and the other cities of southern Idaho.

Large forests cover 40 percent of the state. The manufacture of lumber and wood products, such as fiberboard, plywood, and paper, is an important industry. One of the world's largest white-pine sawmills is at Lewiston. Much hydroelectric power is generated by waterfalls and large dams on rivers.

Tourism is the third most important business. Many people come to ski in winter, especially at Sun Valley in the Sawtooth Mountains. Others come to boat, fish, and hunt. The mining industry earns almost as much as tourism. Idaho mines more silver than any other state. Silver is the state's chief mineral; lead and zinc are next.

▶▶▶▶ **FIND OUT MORE** ◀◀◀◀
Fur; Lewis and Clark Expedition; Shoshone Indians

ILLINOIS

"By thy rivers gently flowing, Illinois, Illinois, By thy prairies verdant growing, Illinois." So the state song of Illinois begins by praising the beauty of the land.

The Land and Climate

Rivers help to give the state its shape. The Mississippi River forms its long western boundary. The Wabash River flows in the southeast between Illinois and Indiana. The Ohio River separates Illinois from Kentucky in the south.

Illinois comes to a point where the Ohio River joins the Mississippi River. The southernmost part of the state, with its rivers and streams, made people think of Egypt near the mouth of the Nile, so they began calling this area "Egypt." The Egypt of Illinois has a city named Cairo, as the real Egypt has. (In Illinois, however, people say "KAYro" instead of "KYro.") Illinois' Egypt, like the one in Africa, also has cities called Thebes and Karnak.

Many rivers flow within the state, too. The main one is the Illinois. This river with other rivers and canals make up the 325-mile (520-km) Illinois Waterway. Boats and barges use this waterway between the Mississippi River and Lake Michigan.

Another river, the St. Lawrence, acts as an outlet for goods from Illinois. The St. Lawrence Seaway, which flows mainly through Canada, connects Chicago and other Great Lakes ports with the Atlantic Ocean.

Illinois' nickname is the "Prairie State." Settlers who came to this region south of the Great Lakes found the grassland, known as prairie, nestled between the wooded river valleys. The grass was waist high. Bright wildflowers grew in it. More than half of Illinois was grassland then. The prairie soil proved to be rich. It is rich because grass plants lived and died in it for thousands of years. The decaying roots of the grass put a great deal of plant food into the soil.

▶ Illinois children voted the violet as the state flower in 1908.

STATE SYMBOLS

▼ The popular cardinal is also the state bird for six other states.

◀ The white oak tree's acorns feed many hungry wild animals.

◀ The bald eagle stands for the U.S.A.

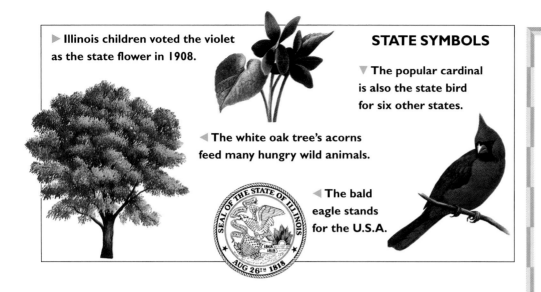

ILLINOIS

Capital
Springfield
(105,227 people)

Area
56,400 square miles
(146,075 sq. km)
Rank: 24th

Population
11,430,602 people
Rank 6th

Statehood
December 3, 1818
(21st state admitted)

Principal river
Illinois River

Highest point
Charles Mound:
1,241 feet (378 m)

Largest city
Chicago
(2,783,726 people)

Motto
State Sovereignty—
National Union

Song
"Illinois"

Famous people
Abraham Lincoln,
Walt Disney

▲ Charles Mound
1,235 ft.
376 m.

© 1994 GeoSystems, an R.R. Donnelley & Sons Company

▶ An aerial photograph showing the vast farmlands of Illinois. The crop being harvested here is soybeans. Illinois grows more soybeans than any other state.

Chicago has three airports, including O'Hare International, which is one of the busiest in the world. The city has museums, an aquarium, a planetarium, and an art institute, as well as colleges, universities, and many hospitals. Chicago handles more freight trains than any other city in the world.

Almost all of the prairie grass is gone now. But the rich soil remains, and the Illinois plain is very good for farming. When you fly over the state, you see broad areas of cropland divided into large, straight-sided fields.

Illinois has no mountain walls to protect it from storm winds. The storms of winter and spring give the state much snow and rain. Northern Illinois is colder in winter than the southern part of the state. But summer weather is about the same in both sections. It is sunny and hot. Summer rain comes largely in thunderstorms. Strong whirling winds called *tornadoes* sometimes strike in spring and summer.

History

Native Americans who lived in the Illinois region in ancient times built thousands of great earthen mounds as burial places or bases for temples. The largest Native American mound in the United States stands in southwestern Illinois. It is in Cahokia Mounds State Park. This mound is a flattened pyramid. It covers 16 acres (6.5 hectares) and is 100 feet (30 m) high in one place. Smaller mounds are found nearby.

The first white people in Illinois were the French. They were members of a small exploring party from New France (Canada), led by Louis Joliet and Father Jacques Marquette, a priest. The party floated down the Mississippi River to the mouth of the Arkansas River in 1673.

In what is now Illinois, the Native Americans were friendly. The principal Native Americans of the region belonged to six united tribes. They called themselves *Illiniwek*. The name was hard for the French to pronounce. So they called the Native Americans "Illinois."

The French lost the French and Indian War in 1763 and gave up the area to Great Britain. Virginian troops under Colonel George Rogers Clark captured it for the United States during the Revolutionary War. Virginia then claimed the Illinois region and other lands next to it. But Virginia turned the land over to the United States government after the Revolution. The Illinois region became part of a large area called the Northwest Territory in 1787. Congress made it part of the Indiana Territory in 1800. The population of settlers in this region grew during the following years. Many Illinois Native

Americans were angry because they were forced by settlers to leave their lands. They fought with the British against the Americans in the War of 1812. Some of these same Native Americans later fought the bitter Black Hawk War in 1832 to keep their lands. They were defeated and forced to leave Illinois.

Illinois became a state in 1818. People from the East and South settled there. Abraham Lincoln and his family came from Kentucky in 1830 after having lived some years in Indiana. Abraham, the oldest son, was 21 at the time. Illinois has become known as the "Land of Lincoln."

New Salem State Park today has a village of log houses. All but one are new. They were built to show what New Salem was like in the 1830s, when Lincoln worked and studied there. Lincoln later moved to the state capital, Springfield, to practice law.

A group of Mormons (members of the Church of Jesus Christ of Latter Day Saints) were among the settlers who came to Illinois in the 1830s. They were seeking religious freedom. The Mormons settled on the banks of the Mississippi River in 1839 and founded the city of Nauvoo there. The city soon became the largest in the state, and Mormons became active in state politics. Other citizens began to resent them. They killed Joseph Smith, the founder of the Mormon church, and drove the Mormons out of Illinois.

An important part of the history of Illinois is the history of its largest city, Chicago. It already covered 18 square miles (29 sq. km) in Lincoln's time. Most of the houses were wood. Chicago was almost entirely destroyed by a great fire in 1871. In 1886, Chicago's Haymarket Square was the scene of a famous, bloody riot by striking workers. The World's Columbian Exposition, held in Chicago in 1893, introduced new ideas, such as electric transit systems and skyscrapers.

Illinois later began the period of its greatest growth. It soon became one of the busiest and richest states in the Union, and it remains one today.

Working in Illinois

Many factories are located in and around Chicago, the state's largest manufacturing center. Other cities, such as Rockford, Peoria, and Decatur, have numerous factories, too.

Several advantages have helped make Illinois a leading manufacturing state. The state has coal and petroleum. Waterways bring fuel and raw materials to factory centers. They carry away manufactured goods. Ocean freighters, as well as lake boats, dock at wharves on Lake Michigan. An unusually good network of road, rail, and air transportation serves Illinois as well. Chicago is a national hub of transportation.

Illinois's leading industry is manufacturing. Much heavy machinery for farms and industries is produced there. Other important products are appliances, clothing, containers, drugs, bricks, and steel. Illinois is also a major agricultural state; corn, oats, wheat, and soybeans are grown here. Hogs, beef cattle, and sheep are raised in large numbers.

Thousands of tourists come to Illinois each year. Public beaches and parks line Chicago's lakefront, where the heat of the summer sun is made bearable by cooling breezes from Lake Michigan. Plenty of streams and lakes for fishing and boating are found. Many visitors are also attracted to Illinois' historical spots. Besides the places associated with Lincoln, there is the former home of President Ulysses S. Grant in Galena, and the Black Hawk Statue in Lowden Memorial State Park.

▶▶▶▶ **FIND OUT MORE** ◀◀◀◀
Chicago; Clark, George Rogers; Great Lakes; Lincoln, Abraham; Marquette, Jacques and Joliet, Louis; Meat; Mormons; Prairie

▲ The Sears building in Chicago is the world's tallest skyscraper. With 110 stories, it reaches a height of 1,454 feet (443m) and boasts 16,100 windows.

▲ Abraham Lincoln's home in Springfield, Illinois. The house, which is open to the public, is furnished exactly as it was when Lincoln and his family lived there .

▲ **Immigrants at a money exchange counter in New York City in the early 1900s.**

Almost 6.4 million immigrants were admitted to the United States in the ten years from 1970 to 1980. This figure exceeded the number from any other decade in U.S. history, except the years from 1901 to 1910, when 8.8 million arrived at the old immigration center on Ellis Island in New York Bay.

IMMIGRATION

Do you know where your ancestors came from? Unless you are a Native American, your parents, grandparents, or great-grandparents probably came to America from across the Atlantic or Pacific oceans. This process is called *immigration*, and the person who comes to a country is called an *immigrant* to that country. The opposite of this is called *emigration*. One who leaves a country is called an *emigrant* from that country.

Nearly 50 million people have immigrated to America's shores. Many people came during two major time periods. The first one, the *old immigration*, began in 1620 and lasted roughly until 1860. Most of these immigrants came from northern Europe. The second period, called the *new immigration*, took place from 1880 to 1920, mostly from southern and eastern Europe and Asia. During that time, more than 27,500,000 new people arrived. Between the old immigration and the new immigration, hundreds of thousands of Asian immigrants landed on America's Pacific coast.

Ancient peoples moved across the

▶ *The Last of England* was painted to symbolize the mass emigration from Europe during the 1800s.

earth to find their food. This movement of peoples is called *migration*. When Europe's nations were forming in the 1500s, and national boundaries were created, migration changed to immigration.

Why did people migrate? To find a better life. Many left crowded European countries for the less populated lands of America. Here, an individual had a better chance to succeed in life. Many came to America to find religious freedom. Others came because rulers told them they could not express their beliefs, vote, or take part in government. Some traveled over many miles of land, then took a dangerous sea journey. Some saved for years to pay for their sea passage.

Throughout most of its history, the United States has welcomed immigrants. Immigrants helped to settle the land and supplied cheap labor for industries. But eventually opposition arose. People who were already living in the U.S. feared that these new immigrants would take jobs and land, and make the country too crowded. In 1882, the Chinese were forbidden to immigrate to the U.S. In 1910, the Japanese were restricted. In 1924, Congress imposed the first *national origins quota* on immigration. This limited the number of immigrants from each country to 2 percent of the number of people of that nationality already living in the United States in 1910. In 1929, Congress further limited the number of immigrants to 150,000 a year, with more immigrants allowed from some countries than from others. In 1965, this system was abolished. The opportunity to immigrate is now first given to relatives of U.S. citizens, to professionals and to political refugees. The 1990 Immigration Act was introduced to clarify and increase the limitations on immigration into the United States.

▶▶▶▶ **FIND OUT MORE** ◀◀◀◀
Citizenship; Statue of Liberty; Ellis Island

IMMUNITY

When you were very young, your doctor probably gave you a vaccination to protect you against the disease called polio, which was once one of our worst enemies. A surprising fact about the polio vaccination is that it probably contained living polio germs! You caught only a very mild case of polio, because these germs were treated to make them harmless. But the germs "trick" your body into acting as if dangerous polio germs have entered your bloodstream, so

your body goes to work fighting them.

Antibodies are special substances that have an important job. They attack certain disease-causing germs in your body. When you get a disease, your body begins to produce antibodies. When these substances kill the disease germs in your body, you get better. Then the antibodies remain in your body to stop more of the same kind of germs from invading your body again. Each type of antibody works against only one type of disease-causing germ.

Long-term protection against dis-

ease is called *immunity*. People have *natural* immunity to many diseases. For example, you will never hear of a person suffering from distemper (a disease that attacks dogs) or from rust (a disease that attacks many kinds of plants). Living conditions inside the human body are not good for these germs. Some people have stronger natural immunity to a disease than other people. Do you remember the last time that an *epidemic* (a disease that spreads very rapidly) happened in your town? Many people got sick, but some people did not get sick at all. Your natural immunity to a certain disease determines whether you get the disease when you are exposed to its germs and just how sick the disease makes you. The Eskimos and Native Americans of North America had no natural immunity to influenza, for example.

People also develop an *acquired* immunity to disease, because they have had the disease and the body produces antibodies that fight off the disease germs if they are exposed to them again. However, the virus that causes AIDS (Acquired Immune Deficiency Syndrome) damages the body's natural immune system, leaving little hope of recovery.

When a doctor gives you a vaccination, he or she injects *antigens* (specially treated germs) into your body. These antigens cause your body to produce antibodies, which keep you from getting the disease. Today, many diseases that were once great dangers

▲ **Louis Pasteur at his clinic. He was one of the first to understand the link between some diseases and germs.**

▲ **Antibody cells are sometimes called memory cells. Once they have met an antigen, they never forget it. When such a cell meets the same antigens (1) it joins onto them (2) and puts them out of action until they are eaten by macrophages (3). The cell then makes copies of itself (4), called plasma cells. These release antibodies into the bloodstream (5), where they attach to the antigens and attract macrophages (6).**

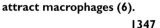

1347

In 1974, the House Judiciary Committee recommended a bill of impeachment against U.S. President Richard Nixon, charging him with breaking the law. Nixon resigned, however, before the House of Representatives voted on it.

Art critics in the 1870s were horrified at the way the Impressionists painted. One critic described how people rocked with laughter at the paintings of artists such as Monet and Degas. He thought the artists were a group of lunatics.

▼ *Boulevard des Italiens, Morning, Sunlight,* by Camille Pissarro. National Gallery of Art, Washington, D. C., Chester Dale Collection.

are not so threatening because nearly all people are immunized to them. With the help of vaccination, smallpox has been wiped out.

However, with certain diseases such as the common cold, your body stops making antibodies almost as soon as the disease is over. Sometimes the germ causing the disease alters slightly so the antibodies no longer work properly. About 150 different viruses have been found that cause the common cold. To date, doctors have not been able to find a vaccination for the common cold.

▶▶▶▶ **FIND OUT MORE** ◀◀◀◀
Antigen and Antibody; Childhood Diseases; Disease; Virus

IMPEACHMENT

The United States Constitution says that a U.S. government official can be removed from office if he or she is convicted of "treason, bribery, and other high crimes and misdemeanors." *Impeachment* is the act of accusing a government official of such a crime. The House of Representatives has the power to impeach a Presi-

dent, Vice President, or other federal official. The Senate then acts as a court to try the official. A two-thirds vote of the Senate is required for conviction. If impeached persons are found guilty, they lose their government jobs and may never hold public office again. But they cannot be fined or imprisoned unless they are also convicted by a regular court of law.

Impeachment has been voted by the House of Representatives 12 times in its history. Nine of these cases involved federal court judges. The other three cases involved a senator, a cabinet member, and a President—Andrew Johnson. Only 4 of the 12 impeached persons were found guilty—all of them judges.

Andrew Johnson, the 17th President of the United States, was Abraham Lincoln's Vice-President and became President in 1865 when Lincoln was assassinated. Johnson had many disagreements with Congress over the treatment of the conquered South after the Civil War. Congress wanted to punish the South, but Johnson did not. Congress passed a law in 1867 that a President could not dismiss a U.S. government employee unless the Senate approved. Johnson dismissed his Secretary of War, Edwin M. Stanton, later that year. The House of Representatives voted to impeach Johnson on February 24, 1868. Johnson's trial by the Senate lasted almost three months. He was found not guilty.

State officials can also be impeached and tried by state legislatures.

▶▶▶▶ **FIND OUT MORE** ◀◀◀◀
Johnson, Andrew

IMPRESSIONISM

In the 1860s in France, a few young artists began a new kind of painting. At that time, most artists worked in their studios, but these people began to paint outdoors. They were interested in light—how it changed and its visual effect on the things they painted. They painted landscapes from nature, where changing light would make it necessary to paint quickly.

In May 1874, the group held its own art show in Paris. The artists were laughed at, and newspaper writers made fun of their paintings. One newsman poked fun at *Impression: Sunrise* by Claude Monet, a leader of the group, and called these artists *Impressionists*. The name stuck, and the new art movement had a name—*Impressionism*.

Another Impressionist, and a friend of Monet, was Camille Pissarro. Pissarro was so eager to paint the Paris streets at various times of day that he rented a hotel room high above two famous Paris boulevards. From the same room, he painted twelve views of the Boulevard Montmartre and two views of the Boulevard des Italiens. He did very different paintings at each time of day.

Notice the early morning shadows and the winter sun starting to creep into the right of the picture on page 1348. This scene is largely painted in neutral tones—a tan street, gray sidewalks, pinkish buildings. Some things seem to be black, but look closely and you will see they are dark brown, green, or blue. Impressionists used no black, which is the absence of light. Touches of bright color show in the horsedrawn buses, the carriage wheels, and clothes of the moving people. Pissarro did not paint a single, neutral blended tone on his canvas. Rather, he put on tiny strokes of complementary colors. He would dab orange next to blue, for example, green next to red, and yellow next to purple. The side-by-side colors fuse in the eye of the viewer at a normal viewing distance. The effect is a sparkle that does not happen when two complementary colors are mixed to make a neutral one.

Pissarro also got the effect of end-

▲ *Regatta at Argenteuil*, by Claude Monet, housed in the Louvre, Paris.

▼ *Les Parapluies* ("Umbrellas") by Pierre Auguste Renoir, housed in the National Gallery, London

less movement with his quick, short painting strokes. Every carriage and each person in the painting is caught in a moment of action. Pissarro's Impressionist approach turns a rather colorless scene into a shimmering landscape of movement.

Regatta at Argenteuil was painted by Claude Monet in 1874, the same year as the Impressionists' exhibition. Imagine Monet, probably at the end of a pier, hanging onto his easel in a stiff breeze, painting a sailboat race! Using techniques similar to those of Pissarro, Monet has caught the impression of a moment in time.

▶▶▶▶ **FIND OUT MORE** ◀◀◀◀

Cassatt, Mary; Degas, Edgar; Gauguin, Paul; Manet, Édouard; Monet, Claude; Renoir, Pierre-Auguste; Toulouse-Lautrec, Henri de; Van Gogh, Vincent

LEARN BY DOING

See for yourself—as the Impressionists did—how light changes your view of an object. Look at a tree in your yard, a rough-textured garage, or a building across the street. Study it in early morning. How long are the shadows from it? Is it in shade? Look at it in the bright noonday sun again just before sunset. What time of day would you most like to paint a picture of it?

INCA

INCA

When the Spanish conquistadors arrived in South America in the 1500s, they found the Inca Empire. The center of this great civilization was located in what is now Peru. The rest of the empire stretched across the western coast of South America in parts of present-day Argentina, Bolivia, Chile, Ecuador, and Colombia. This land was inhabited by six to eight million natives of various tribes. The capital of the empire, Cuzco, was a beautiful city of temples and palaces of stone and gold. The Incas ruled over this empire for more than four centuries.

The Inca Civilization

A great network of stone roads connected all parts of the empire. Since there were no wheeled vehicles or horses, these roads were traveled by swift runners who provided an efficient communications system. The runners memorized messages and used a system of knotted strings to pass on information because the Incas had no writing system. Post houses were located along the roads for the runners, who worked in a relay system. Each person ran a few miles, then gave the message to a fresh runner. The relay system could cover up to 300 miles (500 km) a day. In times of war or during a rebellion of one of the conquered tribes, armies could travel quickly over these roads to all parts of the empire. Storehouses along the way contained provisions for the soldiers. There were also inns where travelers could stop and rest.

The Incas built sturdy suspension bridges over wide ravines and canyons. Some of these rope bridges are still being used today. Other remarkable engneering achievements included vast temples, palaces, and stone fortresses. The stones were carefully cut to enable them to fit together, since the Incas had no cement or other mortar. The stones were so well fitted that a knife blade could not be inserted between them. The Incas also built canals and aqueducts to bring water to their fields.

INCA LIFE. Most of the Incas were farmers. Their language was Quechua, which is still spoken today by the natives of the Andes. A farmer and his family lived in a stone hut, which had only one windowless room. They had llamas and alpacas to carry light loads to markets. There, they would trade their fresh vegetables for meat and cloth. The Incas kept dogs as pets, and ducks and guinea pigs for food.

The Inca government believed that people worked for the state, but the state was responsible for the care of each of its citizens. Government

▶ In the Inca empire, relay runners acted as "mailmen." They carried official messages and packages. Each runner blew into a shell to announce his approach.

▼ To grow crops, the Incas had to cut terraces out of the steep slopes of the Andes. They then harvested the crops with a wooden digging stick called a *taclla*.

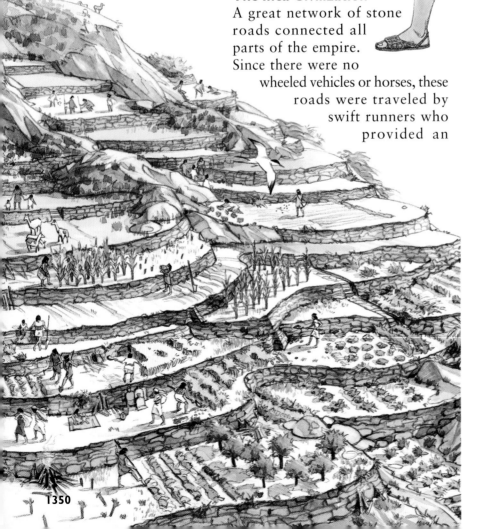

officials taught the farmers how to build stone terracing, and how to fertilize, irrigate, and drain their fields. An irrigation ditch carried water from a nearby stream. The most important crops were corn and potatoes. A part of each grain harvest was stored in warehouses to be used in times of famine.

Some Incas were skilled metal workers. They made metal tools and weapons. They used gold to decorate their temples and palaces and to make beautiful jewelry. Ceramic pottery and woven cloth were also made by skilled craftspeople.

SCIENTIFIC ACHIEVEMENTS. The Inca astronomers charted the solar system and worked out the time for the planting and harvesting of crops. Most medicines were made from herbs or the organs of animals. These were boiled and put into the sick person's food. The Incas were the first to discover that quinine helped in the treatment of malaria.

The Inca number system was based on 10. Population figures and other important statistics were recorded on *quipus*. A *quipu* is a long fiber rope with shorter ropes hanging from it. These hanging ropes were of different colors and could be tied into knots. A knot could stand for 1, 10, 100, or any multiple of 10. Using the quipu, the Incas managed to keep records not only of population figures and crop yields, but also of historical events and daily activities.

THE INCA GOVERNMENT. The Inca emperor was the supreme ruler. The people believed that he was descended from the sun god. In rank below the emperor were the royal family, nobles, government administrators, soldiers, craftspeople, farm laborers, and slaves taken from conquered tribes.

The entire empire was divided into four regions, or units. These regions were subdivided into various smaller regions, and the smallest unit was the farmland worked by a family. Government planners often moved and resettled whole populations for political and economic reasons. Government officials were in charge of each region, and the official of a small region would be under the supervision of the official of the next largest region. These officials were responsible not only for the work done in their regions, but also for the well-being of every person under their management. This extremely efficient method of governing and the Inca communications system enabled the emperor and other officials in Cuzco to exercise firm control over all parts of the empire.

The Incas' system of law and justice was very stern but fair. If persons stole because they were greedy, they would be sentenced to a horrible death. But if persons stole because their families were hungry, they might just be fined a small amount, and the official who was responsible for their village would be punished.

The Fall of the Inca Empire

This was the fabulous Indian empire that Francisco Pizarro and his 177 soldiers saw in 1532. The Incas had never before seen white people, guns, or horses, and they treated the Spaniards as gods.

Pizarro returned their welcome by kidnapping the emperor, Atahualpa. The Incas offered a huge ransom of gold and silver for the return of their emperor. Pizarro took the ransom, and then ruthlessly killed Atahualpa. Without an emperor to lead them, the great Inca army was powerless against the gunpowder of the Spaniards. In this way, the Spaniards gained control of the Inca Empire. They allowed a new emperor to be crowned, but he no longer had any power. Most of the people were forced to work for the spaniards in the gold and silver

▼ An Inca gold model of a llama. Llamas were used for carrying people and packs.

The Incas were the first people to cultivate potatoes. They even invented a way of preserving them by freezing thin slices and then extracting the water. The same basic process is used today to make "instant" mashed potato.

▲ Pots, even elaborate ones, were still made of clay coils until the late 1500s.

During the time of the great Inca empire, the word "Inca" only referred to the nobility and those of royal blood.

▲ **Americans throughout the United States celebrate Independence day with parties and fireworks.**

It was on Independence day, 1884, that the United States received the gift of the Statue of Liberty from the people of France.

mines and the farmlands soon fell into ruin. Many laborers died of overwork and starvation. The last Inca emperor was beheaded by the Spanish in 1571, and the Inca Empire disintegrated.

▶▶▶▶ **FIND OUT MORE** ◀◀◀◀
Ancient Civilizations; Civilization; Conquistadors; Native American Art; Native Americans; Peru; Pizarro, Francisco

INCUBATOR

Chicken eggs will not hatch if they are not kept at a warm temperature of about 99° to 100°F (37.2° to 37.7°C) for 18 to 21 days. In nature, a hen provides the warmth by sitting on the eggs in her nest. Large poultry farms that raise chickens to be sold in markets hatch the eggs in an *incubator*.

A large incubator may hold as many as 100,000 eggs. The eggs are kept warm by electric heaters. Special controls keep the air moist, so that the eggs will not become too dry. As the eggs develop into chicks, oxygen is used up. So fresh oxygen is pumped into the incubator.

The ancient Egyptians had incubators in which they could hatch a million eggs a year. Each incubator was a small, low building with double walls of dried mud. At one end of the building was a room in which a fire was kept burning.

Sometimes human babies are born *prematurely*—before they are fully developed. A premature baby can be kept in an incubator until it grows strong and healthy. An incubator for a baby is a crib with a special glass cover. The temperature inside the crib is kept at 80°F (26.7°C) and oxygen mixed with other gases is pumped into the incubator. A premature baby is weak and may catch serious diseases easily. The incubator protects the baby from

▲ **This baby was born prematurely. The incubator offers protection and increases the baby's chance of survival.**

germs and gives the baby a chance to grow strong.

▶▶▶▶ **FIND OUT MORE** ◀◀◀◀
Egg; Poultry; Reproduction

INDEPENDENCE DAY

People all over the United States celebrate their country's "birthday" each year on the Fourth of July. This joyous holiday is called Independence Day because on that day, July 4, 1776, the Declaration of Independence was adopted by representatives of America's 13 original colonies. This declaration informed the world that the colonies, which were about to fight for their freedom from Great Britain in the Revolutionary War (1775–1783), were now "free and independent states." On July 8, 1776, the first great celebration of this event took place in Philadelphia, Pennsylvania. Bells rang, cannons were fired, and band music filled the air as a grand parade marched down the main street. In the evening, the people enjoyed feasting, dancing, bonfires, and fireworks.

The custom of celebrating the anniversary of the beginning of the United States spread throughout the growing young country and all its territories and possessions. The Fourth of July became a red, white, and blue day of picnics and parades, speeches, games, athletic contests, and fireworks. Many towns and cities today have community festivities, ending the day with dazzling fireworks displays. The sizzling, hissing, ear-rattling explosions and the glorious flashes of color in the night sky make an exciting finish to Independence Day.

▶▶▶▶ FIND OUT MORE ◀◀◀◀
Declaration of Independence;
Revolutionary War

INDEPENDENCE HALL

Some of the most important events in United States history took place in an old two-story, red-brick building in Philadelphia, Pennsylvania. Independence Hall was the meeting place of the Continental Congress from 1775 to 1781. George Washington was appointed commander-in-chief of the Continental Army there in 1775. The Declaration of Independence was adopted in the east room of the building on July 4, 1776. Four days later the famous Liberty Bell, then hanging in the tower of the hall, was rung to celebrate its adoption.

Independence Hall was built between 1732 and about 1750. A wooden bell tower originally stood on top, but the present tower dates from 1828.

Independence Hall has since been restored to look exactly as it did in 1776. It is now a national historical museum. Visitors to the hall can see the original desk and chair used for signing the Declaration of Independence, portraits of most of the signers, and many historical documents.

Independence Hall is part of Independence National Historical Park, in the heart of downtown Philadelphia. In 1948, Congress established the park to preserve the historical

buildings and surroundings. They wanted visitors to see the buildings that played a part in the founding of the United States.

▶▶▶▶ FIND OUT MORE ◀◀◀◀
Continental Congress; Declaration of Independence; Liberty Bell; Philadelphia; Revolutionary War

INDEX

An index is a list, arranged in alphabetical order, of names, topics, and other factual matter to be found in a book, pamphlet, or other publication. An index is placed at the end of the publication. Each entry in the index contains the number of the page, section, or chapter in which the information appears. Most factual books have indexes.

A telephone book is a kind of index, listing in alphabetical order the names, addresses, and telephone numbers of people in a particular area who have telephones. Dictionaries and encyclopedias are indexes to spelling and language, and to information about areas of human knowledge and the world.

What happens if you want to look up something in a magazine? Magazines do not have indexes at the end of every issue, but every library has copies of the *Reader's Guide to Periodical Literature*. The *Reader's Guide* is an index that lists articles from almost all magazines.

Bb

B-52 Stratofortress, 1/62
Babbage, Charles, 3/**285-6**, 3/285
Babe, Bunyon's ox, 2/163
Babies, incubators, 11/1249
Baboons, 14/1636, 14/1637
Babur, 11/1254
Babylonia, 3/**286-7**, 3/286, 11/1335

Before the British occupied Philadelphia during the Revolutionary War, the Liberty Bell was moved to Allentown, Pennsylvania. It was returned to Independence Hall when the British withdrew.

▲ The tower of Independence Hall in Philadelphia. It was here that the Liberty Bell proclaimed the Declaration of Independence.

 A section taken from the index at the end of an encyclopedia showing where the entries are located.

Indexes are not found only in books. Card files are a kind of index. The card or computer catalog in a library is an index of all the books in that library. Many business firms keep indexes, or *inventories*, that show what items are in their storerooms. Today these are often computerized. Computers can be used for a new type of index. A computer can collect and organize information quickly.

▶▶▶▶ **FIND OUT MORE** ◀◀◀◀
Bibliography; Catalog; Library;
Reference Book

INDIA

The republic of India is the seventh largest country in the world. It is about one-third the size of the United States, but has more than three times as many people as the United States does. China is the only country whose population is larger than India's. Overcrowding becomes worse in India each year because the population increases rapidly.

▲ A movie theater in the busy city of New Delhi. Movies are very popular in India, where there is a thriving movie industry.

Geography and Climate

India is called a *subcontinent* because its land area juts away from the Asian mainland into the Indian Ocean. The giant Himalayan Mountains stand along India's northern border with China, Nepal, and Bhutan. Kachenjunga, India's tallest mountain, 28,208 feet (8,598 m) high, is located there. Pakistan lies to the west of India, and Bangladesh and Burma are to the east. Three great rivers, the Indus, Ganges, and Brahmaputra, are supplied by Himalayan snows and glaciers. A wide plain lies south of the Himalayas, stretching between the Arabian Sea on the west and the Bay of Bengal on the east. The soil here is very fertile. The Deccan plateau lies south of this plain. It is separated from the coasts by mountains, called the Eastern Ghats and the Western Ghats.

Throughout much of India, the year is divided into three distinct seasons. The first season lasts from December to March. It is cool and dry, and the winds blow from the northeast across the Asian mainland. The second season, during April and May, is hot and dry. The third season, beginning in June, is rainy. This is the time of the *monsoon*, when strong winds bring heavy rain.

Natural Resources

Rice, one of India's main crops, is grown in the Ganges River valley, along the coasts, and near rivers in the southern part of the country. Wheat, corn, and barley are raised in the northern part of India. Tea shrubs are grown in the moist, northeastern region called Assam. Cotton is grown in the drier southern and central areas. Jute is raised for its fiber, which is used in making rope and sacks. Rubber, pepper, and coffee are grown on plantations. Cashew nuts, coconuts, bananas, and citrus fruits are also raised. India has large deposits of valuable minerals, including high-grade iron ore, coal, mica,

gypsum, manganese, chromite, salt, and oil. India's dense forests contain valuable woods, such as sandalwood, ebony, teak, and bamboo.

India's wildlife is varied. More than 500 species of mammals live there. Indians value the elephant for its ability to do heavy work, such as lumbering. The tigers of India, especially the Bengal tigers, are known all over the world for the beautiful colors of their coats. *Maharajas* (princes) of India hunted this prized animal for sport, as did the British. Fur merchants also hunted tigers, and now these animals are in danger of extinc-

tion. The government has established wildlife sanctuaries in Assam, Karnataka (formerly Mysore), Madras, and other places. These sanctuaries have been set up to preserve the lives of these animals, and no hunting is allowed.

People

India is made up of various regions. The people in each region follow their own customs. They have their own ways of dressing and have developed their own styles of music and dancing. They even have their own languages. In 1956, the Indian government rearranged the state

INDIA

Capital city
New Delhi
(273,000 people)

Area
1,269,346 square miles
(3,287,590 sq. km)

Population
853,373,000 people

Government
Multi-party republic

Natural resources
Coal, bauxite, chromite, gold, iron ore, copper, manganese, mica, titanium, diamonds

Export products
Textiles and clothing, tea, fish, farm products, machinery, coffee, iron ore, gems

Unit of money
Rupee

Official languages
Hindi, English

▶ The Indian emperor Shah Jahān (1627–1657) rebuilt Delhi as the capital of his empire. He spent his last years imprisoned by his treacherous son Aurangzeb.

People marry younger in India than in any other country. The average marrying age for males is 20; for females it is 14½.

boundaries so that most of the people who speak the same language now live in the same state.

India has been called a nation of villages, because most of the people live in small communities. Village life is very important. India is primarily an agricultural nation, and the farm workers must produce enough food to feed India's huge population. Even with the many food products grown in India, the people often go hungry. When there is not enough rainfall, crops do not grow. Many Indians will not eat beef because of their religious belief that the cow is a sacred animal. In order to feed the people, India must import some of its food. Villagers in India are also employed in *cottage industries* where they work at home or in small workshops. Cottage industrial workers process food and make cloth and handicrafts.

Twelve cities in India have populations of more than one million people. They are Calcutta, Bombay, Delhi, Madras, Bangalore, Hyderabad, Ahmadabad, Kanpur, Pune, Nagpur, Lucknow, and Jaipur. Calcutta, the largest city, has nearly eleven million people living in and around it. Madras has large textile mills and is noted for cotton cloth, called *madras*. City workers are employed in large factories where iron and steel, as well as machinery and fertilizer, are manufactured. Thousands of people have come to India's large cities from the country, hoping to find work. The cities now contain vast numbers of unemployed poor who have no food and live in the streets, because there is no place to house them.

Most of India's population lives along the three main river systems: the Indus, Ganges, and Brahmaputra. The Ganges is a holy river for the Hindus. Sacred shrines and temples line its banks. The great majority of Indians are either Hindu or Muslim; a few are Christian, and a few are Buddhist.

History

Indian civilization is about 5,000 years old. Almost 2,500 years before the birth of Christ, a group of people, called Aryans, moved into the Indus River valley from the northwest. They gradually took over most of the northern area of India. Little is known about the people who lived in India before the Aryans came. Perhaps the original settlers were the Dravidians who live in southern India today. They are usually shorter and have somewhat darker skins than the people living in the north.

When the Aryans arrived in the north, the Dravidians moved to the south. The Aryans created a highly developed civilization. They raised crops and worked with metal tools. Two great religions, Buddhism and Hinduism, developed in India. Hinduism began about 3,000 years ago. Buddhism began in the 500s B.C. and spread to other Asian lands. In 326 B.C., a Greek army, led by Alexander the Great, invaded the Indus River valley region, but did not greatly affect the Aryan civilization. After the Greek invasion, the Aryan people united under Chandragupta, a native Indian ruler, and gained control of most of the country. Chandragupta was the first king of the Maurya dynasty. This *dynasty* (series of rulers belonging to the same family) lasted until 200 B.C. The greatest

▲ Babur, who founded the Mogul empire when he invaded northern India from Afghanistan in 1526, and defeated the sultan of Delhi.

Mauryan emperor, Asoka, became a Buddhist and helped to spread that religion.

Various dynasties held power during the next 300 to 400 years. The Sunga dynasty lasted the longest of these, ruling for more than 100 years. During the Sunga reign, Hinduism replaced Buddhism and again became the main religion. The Hindu *caste system* became widespread. The population was divided into religious *castes* (classes). When people were born, they belonged to the caste of their parents. Throughout their life, they could associate with and marry only people who belonged to their own caste. The caste system is now discouraged, but many Indians still believe in it.

Muslims from the Middle East came to India in the A.D. 700s and set up trading colonies there. They brought their faith, Islam, with them. By the twelfth century, Muslim Turks had conquered all of the Ganges River valley east of Bengal. In 1398, the Mongol conqueror, Tamerlane, entered the country and captured the city of Delhi. For the next hundred years or so, India was an area of many small kingdoms. Then in 1526, Babur, a Muslim and a descendant of Tamerlane, conquered most of the Indian mainland, proclaimed himself emperor, and founded the Mogul dynasty. This dynasty, under the emperors Akbar, Jahangir, and Shah Jahān, encouraged learning, the sciences, and the arts. One of the most beautiful buildings in the world, the Taj Mahal, was built by Shah Jahān.

In the late 1400s, Europeans began searching for new places with which to trade. The Portuguese explorer, Vasco da Gama, discovered a sea route to India in 1498. The Portuguese, Dutch, British, and French all battled for control of the Indian trade. England finally dominated the Indian trade in the 1700s, forming the British East India Company. The Mogul empire collapsed, and the British ruled India as a colony for nearly 200 years under an administration started by Robert Clive, who was called "Clive of India."

India in the Twentieth Century

The Indian people began seeking independence in the late 1800s. In the 1920s, Mohandas (Mahatma) Ghandi became head of the independence movement. He started his civil disobedience campaign of nonviolence in which people peacefully refused to obey British laws. They boycotted elections, schools, and courts, and refused to buy British goods. The British could not rule under such conditions. In 1947, Britain gave up its power in India. Shortly afterward, the regions of India that were mostly Muslim formed the independent nation of Pakistan.

Since then, hostility and outbreaks of fighting have occurred between India and Pakistan. They fought for two years over the territory of Kashmir. After the cease-fire in January 1949, each nation was left in control of about half the territory. In 1971, India and Pakistan began fighting over who would rule East Pakistan. The Indians defeated the Pakistani army and made it possible for the people of East Pakistan to establish the new nation of Bangladesh.

India became a member of the Commonwealth of Nations in 1950.

▶ ▶ ▶ ▶ **FIND OUT MORE** ◀ ◀ ◀ ◀
Asia; Buddhism; Gandhi, Indira; Gandhi, Mahatma; Hinduism; Monsoon; Nehru, Jawaharlal; Pakistan

▲ **An Indian dancer in costume. The positions of the dancer's hands, fingers, and arms tell stories.**

◀ **Hindus and Buddhists believe that life is based on recurring cycles. As a symbol of this, the "wheel of life" is seen in many Buddhist temples.**

▲ **Jawaharlal Nehru, who was the first prime minister of India (1947 until his death in 1964). His daughter, Indira Ghandi, took over in 1966.**

▲ Covered bridges are one of the many picturesque sights of rural Indiana. Parke County has more than 30 covered bridges.

When the Civil War broke out, Indiana offered many more volunteers to the Union than could be accepted. About 100,000 men from Indiana served in the Union forces.

▲ Indiana's first territorial capitol was in Corydon. The only recorded fighting in Indiana, during the Civil War (1861–1865), took place in the town of Corydon.

INDIANA

People from Indiana are often called *Hoosiers*. It is not certain where this word came from. It may have come from the question "Who's yer?" that pioneers asked when a newcomer arrived in the state. Or it may have come from the name of a canal builder, Samuel Hoosier, who lived about 150 years ago. Hoosier hired Indiana men rather than those from other states. He said they worked the best.

Among the well-known Hoosiers are the poet James Whitcomb Riley, and the novelists Booth Tarkington and Theodore Dreiser. The songwriter Cole Porter was a Hoosier, too, as were Presidents Benjamin Harrison and William Henry Harrison.

The Land and Climate

Indiana lies in the plains that curve south around the Great Lakes. To the north are Lake Michigan and the state of Michigan. Illinois is on the west. Ohio is on the east. The Ohio River forms the state's southern boundary with Kentucky.

Most of Indiana is in the basin of the Wabash River. Part of this basin is the valley of the White River, which flows into the Wabash. The soil here is very fertile.

When the early settlers came, most of the state was covered with forests of oak and hickory. The rest was prairie grassland. Today, crops grow where grass used to wave in the wind, and much of the forest has been cut down. Indiana now has several big cities, but fields, meadows, and woods cover 85 percent of its area.

Indiana has two valuable resources under its soil: coal and stone. You may have heard of Indiana limestone. It is used all over the country in the construction of buildings.

Indiana summers are hot, but winds from Lake Michigan keep the heat in the northern sections from being unpleasant. Winters can be very cold. Rainfall is plentiful in Indiana. The state lies where cold air from the north meets warm, moist air from the Gulf of Mexico. The warm air is chilled by the cold. Once the air is cooled, it cannot hold so much moisture, so rain falls.

History

Indiana means "Land of the Indians." Indians (Native Americans) lived in the region long before white people came. They made copper ornaments and built great earthen mounds as burial places or as bases for their temples. No one knows what happened to the ancient mound-building Native Americans. When white people came to Indiana, other tribes were living there. The principal tribe was the Miami. During the 1600s and 1700s, tribes from the East moved into Indiana as Europeans took their lands along the Atlantic coast. French fur traders and Catholic priests were the first white persons to come to the Indiana region. The oldest town, established by the French, is Vincennes, located on the Wabash River. It was founded in the 1730s.

France lost the French and Indian War in 1763, and Great Britain took control of the French-held lands around the Great Lakes. In 1776, the British lost the region south of the lakes in the Revolutionary War. Virginia riflemen, led by Colonel George Rogers Clark, took Vincennes and other fortified places.

By the early 1800s, many American settlers had come into the Great Lakes region. Some Native American chiefs tried to hold onto what was left of their land. Tecumseh, a Shawnee chief, united a number of tribes. His brother, who was called "the Prophet," helped him. The brothers talked with William Henry Harrison, governor of the Indiana Territory. They asked him not to

STATE SYMBOLS

◀ **The cardinal was officially chosen as state bird on March 9, 1933.**

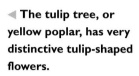

▲ **Indiana's seal shows a pioneer scene. It was officially adopted in 1963.**

◀ **The tulip tree, or yellow poplar, has very distinctive tulip-shaped flowers.**

▶ **The showy peony is widely grown in Indiana.**

INDIANA

Capital and largest city
Indianapolis
(715,000 people)

Area
36,291 square miles
(93,986 sq. km)
Rank: 38th

Population
5,580,000 people
Rank: 14th

Statehood
December 11, 1816
(19th state admitted)

Principal river
Wabash River

Highest point
1,240 feet (378 m), close to the Ohio border

Motto
Crossroads of America

Song
"On the Banks of the Wabash, Far Away"

Famous people
Charles and Mary Beard, Hoagy Carmichael, Theodore Dreiser, David Letterman, Cole Porter, Ernie Pyle, Dan Quayle, Booth Tarkington, Wilbur Wright

© 1994 GeoSystems, an R.R. Donnelley & Sons Company

allow white settlers to take over more land without the consent of the united tribes. They also asked him to give back some of the land that had been bought from the Native Americans. Governor Harrison would not agree. He moved troops toward the Prophet's town near the Tippecanoe River. Tecumseh was away at the time. The Prophet led his warriors in an attack, but they were defeated at the battle of Tippecanoe in 1811. William Henry Harrison later became the ninth President of the United States.

After the War of 1812, nearly all the Native Americans of Indiana were forced to move westward, as white settlers arrived in large numbers. Indiana was made a state in 1816.

The Civil War brought serious problems to Indiana. As a northern state, Indiana backed the Union, but many of its citizens were originally from the South and sided with the Confederacy. The people of the state were divided by the quarrel during and after the war.

Indiana's coal brought wealth to the state. Coal was used in making steel. It was burned by the steam engines that ran factory machines, pulled trains, and turned the paddle wheels of boats. Luckily for Indiana's business executives and farmers, millions of people needed farm and factory equipment. Indiana could produce huge quantities of both. It became a manufacturing state as well as an agricultural state.

Indiana's central location and its trade made transportation very important to the state. Railroads, highways, and airlines serve the state well. Since the opening of the Port of Indiana at Burns Harbor on Lake Michigan in 1970, Indiana has had rapid economic growth. Large oceangoing freighters and other ships coming from the St. Lawrence Seaway dock, unload, and take on cargoes there.

▶ Corn fields in Indiana. Indiana's number-one crop is corn, and this contributes to the state's standing as one of the top ten agricultural states in the nation.

Corydon became Indiana's first state capital in 1813. Indianapolis became the permanent capital in 1825. It was built in the very center of the state.

The famous Indianapolis 500 automobile race takes place every year on the Saturday before Memorial Day. More than 300,000 people attend the race. The first "Indy 500" took place in 1911, and the winning car averaged 74.58 miles per hour (120 km/h). The race is called the "500" because drivers have to complete 200 laps of the 2½-mile (4 km) track—a distance of 500 miles (805 km).

Working in Indiana

Indianapolis is the largest manufacturing center in the state. Fort Wayne, Gary, Evansville, Kokomo, Muncie, and South Bend are important manufacturing cities, too. Indiana turns out billions of dollars' worth of factory equipment and products every year. Machinery is first in value. Metals—

mostly iron and steel—come next. The city of Gary is one of the greatest steel-producing centers in the world. Motor vehicles and other transportation equipment are made in Indiana's factories.

Indiana is also an important agricultural state. Farmers grow corn (the state's main crop), soybeans, wheat, vegetables, and fruits. Much of the corn and other grain crops are fed to hogs and cattle, two valuable livestock products in Indiana. Many sheep, horses, and poultry are also raised in the state.

A popular tourist attraction is Mounds State Park, where the ancient Native American burial mounds can be seen.

▶ ▶ ▶ ▶ **FIND OUT MORE** ◀ ◀ ◀ ◀

Clark, George Rogers; French And Indian War; Great Lakes; Harrison, Benjamin; Harrison, William Henry; Riley, James Whitcomb; Tecumseh; War of 1812

INDIAN ART, AMERICAN

SEE NATIVE AMERICAN ART

INDIAN OCEAN

The Indian Ocean is the third largest ocean in the world. Only the Atlantic and Pacific are bigger. The Indian Ocean touches four continents: Africa is on the west; Asia is the north boundary; in the south and east are Antarctica and Australia, respectively.

Important trade routes cross the northern part of the Indian Ocean. Ships from the Pacific travel across the ocean to reach the Suez Canal and Europe. When the canal is closed, ships must sail around Africa to the Atlantic Ocean. Oil super-tankers crisscross the ocean between the Arab nations of the Persian Gulf and other nations.

The Indian Ocean is more than 4,000 miles (6,400 km) wide at the equator and extends more than 6,000 miles (9,600 km) from north to south. At its deepest point, in the Java Trench, it is 25,344 feet (7,725 m)—almost 5 miles (8 km)—deep.

Several important islands are located in the Indian Ocean. The largest ones are Madagascar, near Africa, and Sri Lanka, just off the tip of India. Other islands include the Seychelles, which attract many tourists because of the warm weather, remote location, and beautiful white sandy beaches.

Much of southeast Asia gets its seasonal weather from the Indian Ocean. Strong winds from the ocean, called *monsoons*, bring moisture deep inland each summer. This seasonal rainfall is needed for crops to grow.

▶▶▶▶ **FIND OUT MORE** ◀◀◀◀
Ocean; Weather

INDIANS, AMERICAN

SEE NATIVE AMERICANS

INDIAN WARS

As colonists settled in the New World, they moved onto Native American hunting grounds. The Native Americans were forced to move or to fight for their lands. Most tribes refused to leave their lands, so many wars were fought, starting in the early 1600s. By the 1890s, most Native Americans in the United States had been resettled on *reservations* (public land set aside for Native Americans).

Both colonists and Native Americans farmed and hunted. But the colonists did not know or care that each tribe thought its land was holy, and that plants and animals contained spirits that had to be respected.

The first major war between the

Toward the end of the Indian Wars, bands of Apaches fought against unbelievable odds. During 1881, fewer than 40 Apache braves fought and won battle after battle against U.S. troops, Texas Rangers, border guards, and ranchers in a campaign that went on for two months. In 1884, less than a dozen Apache warriors raided many miles of enemy territory. They spread terror and *eluded* (escaped from) 2,000 U.S. troops, while losing only one warrior.

▼ **The Creek Chief, Red Eagle, surrendering his land after the Battle of Horseshoe Bend in 1814.**

▲ Born a Mohawk, Joseph Brant (1742–1807) fought on the British side during the French and Indian War. He was given an English name and education.

▲ During the 1800s, many battles took place between Native American tribes and the U.S. army. Often the tribes were outnumbered and could not compete with army weapons.

colonists and Native Americans was fought in Virginia in 1622. By 1641, almost 35 years after the first colonists arrived at Jamestown, the powerful Powhatan tribe was destroyed. In 1637, New England colonists attacked a Pequot settlement in Connecticut and killed all 600 people who lived there. Another New England war began in 1675. King Philip, whose Native American name was Metacomet, was chief of the Wampanoags and a brilliant soldier. He led attacks against several frontier towns in Massachusetts. But Metacomet was killed in 1676, and his people were sold as slaves.

As settlers crossed the Appalachian Mountains, the Native Americans there fought to protect their hunting grounds. Pontiac, a great chief of the Ottawas, led many tribes against the settlers. Pontiac's warriors killed 2,000 settlers and captured ten British forts along the Great Lakes and in Pennsylvania and Virginia. In 1763, Pontiac was defeated by the British and agreed to fight no more.

The Delaware, Shawnee, and Cayuga were defeated in Lord Dunmore's War in 1774. The war was fought because settlers wanted the lands of these Native Americans (now part of Ohio). Additional Ohio territory was captured from the Shawnee, Ottawa, Ojibwa (Chippewa), and Potawatomi after the Battle of Fallen Timbers in 1794. At that battle, nearly 2,000 warriors were crushed by the forces of Major General "Mad Anthony" Wayne.

The last Indian wars to be fought east of the Mississippi River were the Seminole wars, which began in 1817 and did not end until 1858. The Seminoles were forced from their Florida home to a reservation in Oklahoma. Some hid in the swamps of the Everglades, where their descendants still live today.

As Native American lands were taken over by settlers, tribes were pushed westward. Native Americans made treaties with the U.S. government and promised to live peacefully on their reservations, in return for money and goods.

The Sioux and Cheyenne tribes fought many battles against the U.S. Army between 1854 and 1890. The Sioux were brave warriors who used horses in battle, which the eastern tribes had not done. When the Sioux left their Black Hills reservation, General George A. Custer followed. He and the 250 soldiers under his command were killed by the Sioux, who numbered at least 2,000. Chiefs Crazy Horse and Sitting Bull led the Sioux against Custer in the Battle of Little Big Horn, Montana, in 1876. In 1890, avenging soldiers killed hundreds of unarmed Sioux prisoners, including women and children, at Wounded Knee Creek, South Dakota.

The Native Americans of the southern plains—the Cheyenne, Arapaho, Kiowa, and Comanche—also fought for their tribal lands. Battles took place over a period of more than 25 years, from 1865 to 1891. The Nez Percé tribe lived in Idaho. They agreed to move to a reservation, but some settlers stole their horses and war broke out. The Nez Percé chief was named Joseph. His Native American name meant "thunder rolling in the mountains." Joseph led many successful raids on the white soldiers. When he saw that his people could never succeed in holding their lands, he led his whole tribe across 1,000 miles (1,600 km) of mountainous territory toward safety in Canada. When soldiers were finally able to surround the tribe, they were only 30 miles (50 km) south of the Canadian border. They fought the soldiers for five days before surrendering. They were then forced to move to a reservation.

The Navaho and Apache fought U.S. troops in many battles in New Mexico, Arizona, and Texas. The Apaches were brave warriors. Their best-known leaders were Mangas Coloradas, Cochise, and Geronimo. The Apache managed to hold off the troops for 40 years, until 1886 when Geronimo and his followers surrendered. The Apache defeat was the end of the last Indian War.

▶▶▶▶ **FIND OUT MORE** ◀◀◀◀

Apaches; Cherokees; Comanches; Custer, George; French and Indian War; Iroquois; Joseph, Chief; Native Americans; Navajos; Nez Percé; Pontiac; Powhatan; Seminoles; Sioux; Sitting Bull; Westward Movement

INDONESIA

More than 13,500 islands lying southeast of the Asian mainland form the republic of Indonesia. They make up the world's largest island group and fifth most populous country. Java, Sumatra, Celebes, central and southern Borneo, and Irian Jaya are the principal areas. About three-fifths of the people live on the island of Java. The high, mountainous islands of Indonesia have a humid, tropical climate. The rain and warmth make it a colorful country. Beautiful flowers, wild orchids, and ferns are plentiful. Monkeys, tigers, lizards called Komodo dragons, and a rare species of rhinoceros live in Indonesia.

Indonesian families usually live in small villages and grow crops—including rice, sweet potatoes, corn, cassava, soybeans, and coconuts—for a living. Rubber, palm oil, sugarcane, tea, coffee, and tobacco are raised on plantations and are often exported. Forests produce rattan, teakwood, and kapok (used for life preservers and padding).

Indonesia has vast mineral resources that are largely untapped. Petroleum is Indonesia's most important mineral product. Indonesia is one of the world's largest suppliers of tin. Bauxite, coal, nickel, copper, iron ore, and manganese are also mined in the islands.

Indonesian dancing is famous throughout the world. Dancers from Bali are especially famous for their graceful temple dances.

INDONESIA

Capital city
Jakarta
(7,829,000 people)

Area
735,139 square miles
(1,904,000 sq. km)

Population
180,763,000 people

Government
Multi-party republic

Natural resources
Oil, natural gas, lumber, tin, copper, bauxite, nickel, coal, silver, gold

Export products
Oil, gas, lumber, coffee, rubber

Unit of money
Rupiah

Official language
Bahasa Indonesian

▲ **Both the Indonesian princes and the Dutch colonists benefited from the profits made by growing cash crops on the island.**

In 1960, natural rubber accounted for about half of Indonesia's export trade. By 1980, this had fallen to one-fortieth of the total. In the same period, oil and natural gas exports rose from one-fourth to over three-fourths.

▶ **Painting designs on china and pottery is a highly skilled job requiring a good deal of training and patience.**

The Indonesians speak more than 250 languages. Their country's official language is Indonesian, the most widely spoken tongue. About 88 percent of the population are Muslims. But many people living on Bali are Hindus. About 9 percent of the Indonesians are Christians.

Early explorers called Indonesia the Spice Islands. The first Dutch trading ships arrived in the late 1500s. For more than 300 years, the Dutch controlled the islands, known then as the Netherlands East Indies. The Japanese occupied the islands during World War II. Indonesians fought for and won their independence from the Dutch in 1949. Achmed Sukarno, the country's first president, established close ties with Communist China. General Suharto crushed a Communist plot to seize power in 1965. He was elected president in 1968, and reelected in 1973, 1978, 1983, 1988, and 1993.

▶▶▶▶ **FIND OUT MORE** ◀◀◀◀
Asia; Borneo; New Guinea

INDUSTRIAL ARTS

In junior and senior high school, students can learn about making and building things by taking courses in industrial and other arts. These courses teach the *manual skills* (the ability to work expertly with the hands) used in business and industry to make nearly all the products we use.

A course in *industrial drawing and design* teaches students how to *design* (plan) the appearance and structure of anything from an engine to a house. Students learn how the object's parts fit together to make it

work and what materials and tools are needed for its construction. They also learn how to read and to make detailed drawings, called *blueprints*, of the plan.

Students of *woodworking* and *carpentry* learn how to design products, such as chairs or bookcases, that will be functional and show the beauty of a piece of wood. They then learn how to join pieces of wood and other materials together to make the object strong and attractive. Students also learn different ways to finish wood, to protect it, and to give smoothness and shine to the product.

In *metalworking*, students learn how metals are made, including those that combine to make alloys. They also learn how to work with tools used to *machine*, or bend, metals into desired shapes. Students often learn *welding* (joining pieces of metal together, usually with heat) and other machine shop methods.

A course in *electricity and electronics* presents information on how electricity is *generated* (produced) and *transformed* (changed into power) for such things as heat and light. Students also learn how electronics is used for radio, TV, and radar. In this kind of class, students often learn to repair radios, stereos, and television sets.

A course in *auto mechanics* teaches students all the parts of an automobile engine and the way these parts work together. In this course, students

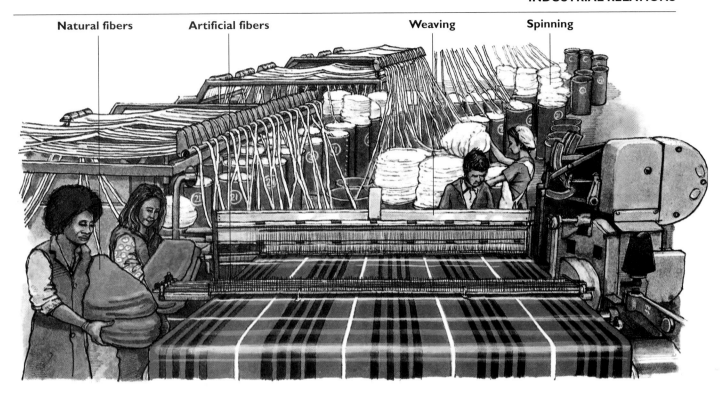

Natural fibers   Artificial fibers   Weaving   Spinning

learn to repair engines and to care for them properly. Some schools offer a course in *electric power mechanics*, in which students are shown how to use machines and motors that operate on electric power.

Graphic arts includes a study of all kinds of printing and photographic methods. Students *layout* (arrange in a design) pages using photographs, type and graphics, such as for a magazine or book.

Students who take courses in *plastics* and *ceramics* learn how to make things out of plastic, clay, concrete, stone, and glass. Students may make something as simple as a bowl or as complicated as a statue.

Many communities provide vocational high schools where students take industrial arts courses to prepare them for jobs in industry immediately after graduation. Students who have learned a specific industrial arts skill are often able to find jobs easily. Mechanics, electricians, and carpenters, for example, frequently get experience working for other people or for large companies before starting their own businesses. Those with metalworking skills may become toolmakers for manufacturing

companies. If a person can read blueprints, he or she may use that skill to build airplanes or to write technical manuals. A person who has studied graphic arts might get a job in a printing shop. Other students go on to technical schools or colleges to improve their skills or to learn new ones before getting a job.

Many people, however, study industrial arts to learn new hobbies. Someone with a knowledge of woodworking may refinish furniture for a hobby. A person with some experience in design and construction and a fondness for sailing might take up boat-building. Others make prints or ceramics in their spare time. A great many people like to take photographs. A knowledge of the industrial arts can prepare a person for a hobby or a career that brings both pleasure and satisfaction.

▶▶▶▶ **FIND OUT MORE** ◀◀◀◀
Architecture; Careers ; Design;
Graphic Arts; Mechanical Drawing

INDUSTRIAL RELATIONS

SEE LABOR UNIONS

▲ **A course in textiles teaches students about natural fibers, such as wool and cotton, and artificial fibers, such as nylon. Students will learn the appropriate uses for all types of materials, as well as how to spin and weave them.**

▶ The weaving industry saw some of the first factory automation with the Jacquard loom.

Cotton gin

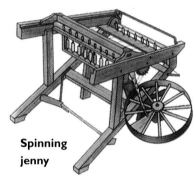

Spinning jenny

▲ Machines used in the cotton industry were among the first to adapt to steam.

▼ Many people left the villages and moved to crowded towns that had grown up around factories.

INDUSTRIAL REVOLUTION

People have always manufactured weapons, tools, clothing, and other goods that they need. For many centuries, these things were made mostly by hand. They were manufactured in the home or by individual craftspeople. Most people also produced their own food on farms. About 200 years ago, this system began to change. People began to produce manufactured goods in large quantities in factories. They did not have time to tend their farms, and so they began to buy their food in stores. This great change in the way people lived is called the *Industrial Revolution*.

England was the birthplace of this revolution. In that country, where *textiles* (cloth) were a major source of wealth, a new method of manufacturing was started, called the *domestic system*. Merchants would distribute large quantities of wool to be spun and woven by the people who wished to earn money by working in their homes. The merchants then paid the people for their work and sold the cloth at a profit.

In the mid-1700s, a Scotsman, James Watt, invented the first workable steam engine. This invention created a vast new source of power. A machine was invented that could spin several threads at one time.

Then a mechanical loom was perfected for weaving the thread. The machines made large quantities of a product quickly and very cheaply. This process became known as *mass production*. The merchants who had grown rich from the domestic system began to buy the new machines. They built factories to house the machines, and employed workers to run them. By the mid-1800s, hundreds of factories had been built in England. Machines were also invented for making other products, such as pottery. The making of the machines themselves became a major industry.

It was not long before the Industrial Revolution began to spread from Britain to other countries. Despite attempts by the British government to prohibit the export of machinery and craftsmen, the textile industries of other European countries and the United States were soon being modernized. An American businessman, Francis Cabot Lowell, established one of the first modern textile factories in Waltham, Massachusetts. Soon the new industrial processes were well established.

Large amounts of iron were needed to make the new machines. Charcoal had always been used to *smelt* (melt) iron ore. But iron workers now discovered that iron ore could be smelted much more efficiently

with coal. The mining industry grew with the need for coal and ore. A method soon was discovered for making steel from iron. Much stronger and more accurate machines could be made from this new metal. Manufactured goods and raw materials had to be transported to and from the factories. The shipping industry flourished. Railroads, canals, and new roads were built. The telegraph was invented, quickly speeding up the communications industry.

As the Industrial Revolution spread throughout Europe and the United States, people's lives began to change. The factories created many new jobs. But they also took some jobs away, by replacing people with machines. People came from far away to work in the factories, hoping to make more money than they could on the farms. They crowded into the new towns that were growing up around the factories. Living conditions were terrible in these towns. People had to work long hours, often in dangerous conditions. They were paid very little money. Many women and children were employed, even in the mines. Workers began to rebel against these injustices. They formed groups that were later called *labor unions*. They gathered to protest against their employers, and sometimes fights broke out, with violence on both sides. Eventually, laws were passed to correct many of the harsh working conditions, and the unions gained great strength.

The Industrial Revolution brought enormous wealth and power to England, parts of Europe, and the United States. But this wealth and power was mainly in the hands of the people who owned the industries.

Today, other nations throughout the world are going through their own industrial revolutions. The change from an agricultural to an industrial economy can now take place rather quickly. Modern industry has raised the standard of living in many countries, but it has also created many serious problems. Factory work is often dull and unrewarding, and workers need more responsibility. Too many people are still crowded into the cities. Waste products of factories have polluted the air and the water. But industry and governments everywhere are aware of these problems and are using scientific methods to improve the kind of life people can have in a modern, industrial society.

In recent years, the development of the microchip and the computer have created a new kind of revolution in technology, industry, and commerce—a modern successor to the Industrial Revolution.

▶ ▶ ▶ ▶ **FIND OUT MORE** ◀ ◀ ◀ ◀
Air Pollution; Capitalism; Child Labor; City; Coal; Fulton, Robert; Iron and Steel; Labor Union; Manufacturing; Petroleum; Stocks and Bonds; Water Pollution; Watt, James; Whitney, Eli

INFECTION

SEE DISEASE

INFLATION

SEE ECONOMICS

▲ In the early 1800s, steam was harnessed to pull trains. This picture of 1830 shows second-class carriages on the Liverpool-Manchester line in northwest England.

The Industrial Revolution began in Britain, but after a time it spread to Europe and the United States. Between 1810 and 1812, an American named Frances Cabot Lowell visited textile mills in Lancashire, England and returned to the United States to set up a textile factory. This factory was one of the first in the world to combine all the processes for making cotton cloth under one roof.

QUIZ

1. What country was the birthplace of the Industrial Revolution?
2. Who invented the first workable steam engine?
3. What is *mass production*?
4. Where in the United States was one of the first modern textile factories?
5. What were the conditions like in the first factory towns?

(Answers on page 1408)

INFRARED

SEE HEAT AND COLD

☼ INK

Whenever you read anything that is printed, such as a newspaper, book, or poster, you are reading something printed with ink. If you write with a pen, you are writing with ink. Ink is any liquid used for writing or printing. The first inks, thousands of years ago, were probably made from the juice of several kinds of berries.

▼ **Chinese ink makers preparing and mixing the ingredients (soot, resin, oil, and gum). The Chinese began making ink around 1500 B.C.**

There are many kinds of ink, and most of them are made of *dyes* (coloring materials) dissolved in liquid. The kind of dyes and liquids used depends on what an ink is to be used for. For example, the ink used in ballpoint pens is a thick, jellylike liquid. A ballpoint pen puts very little ink on paper, so the dye in the ink must have a very strong color. On the other hand, ballpoint ink would not work in a fountain pen. Fountain pen ink is more watery.

The liquid part of most printing inks dries very quickly. This quick drying is necessary because paper moves through modern printing presses very fast. Immediately after printing, the paper is stacked, cut, and folded. The ink would smear and run if it did not dry rapidly.

Invisible, or *sympathetic*, ink becomes invisible when it dries. Something must then be done to the dried ink to make it visible. It may be dipped in, or sprayed with, chemicals, or it may be heated. Invisible ink used to be a favorite of spies, but the modern ways of making invisible ink visible make it too easy to be read.

▶▶▶▶ **FIND OUT MORE** ◀◀◀◀
Dye; Printing

INQUISITION

SEE SPANISH HISTORY

▨ INSECT

Insects make up about four-fifths of all the animals on Earth. More than 900,000 kinds of insects are known, and *entomologists*—scientists who study insects—discover about 7,000 new kinds of insects each year.

Insects' Survival

There are several reasons why insects are so plentiful. First, they are able to live in every kind of environment. Insects live in every part of the Earth, including the coldest polar regions, the hottest deserts, and the middle of the ocean. They live everywhere outdoors, and also in every kind of human dwelling place, from grass huts to brick apartment houses.

Second, most insects are small, needing little space and little food. About 21 acres (8.5 hectares) of the Earth's surface grow only enough

---

LEARN BY DOING

You can make invisible ink by writing your message with lemon juice. The writing will disappear as soon as it dries. But you can see the message again by placing the paper on a warm radiator for a few minutes.

food for one human being for a year, but the same space can feed more than a billion insects. One bread crumb can provide a day's food for several ants. Most insects eat plants or other insects. Termites eat wood. Some insects, such as mosquitoes, live on the blood of human beings and other animals.

Third, insects reproduce very rapidly. For example, a single house-fly lays 120 to 160 eggs. The eggs hatch in a few hours, and in three to six days these flies are full grown, ready to produce another generation.

Harmful Insects

Fortunately, only a few of the hundreds of thousands of kinds of insects are harmful to people. Perhaps the greatest harm is done by crop-eating insects, which destroy millions of tons of grains, vegetables, and fruits every year. Locusts and other grasshoppers destroy plants by eating the leaves. The larvae of many insects eat leaves and stems. Cutworms and corn borers, the larvae of two different moths, feed on many field crops. The larvae of Colorado beetles damage potatoes. Gypsy moth and tussock moth larvae can leave acres of trees without leaves.

A number of insects are household pests. Clothes moths damage wool clothes. Silverfish damage clothes, books, and leather. Weevils live in flour and other foods, and cockroaches invade all kinds of food.

Some insects carry serious diseases from one person to another, or from animals to people. Certain mosquitoes carry malaria and yellow fever. Rat fleas carry bubonic plague. Lice carry typhus. Ordinary houseflies carry more than 40 serious diseases including typhoid, cholera, and dysentery.

Many insect pests can be controlled by using *insecticides*. (The suffix "-cide" means "killer of.") Insecticides that destroy crop-eating insects have helped to increase the

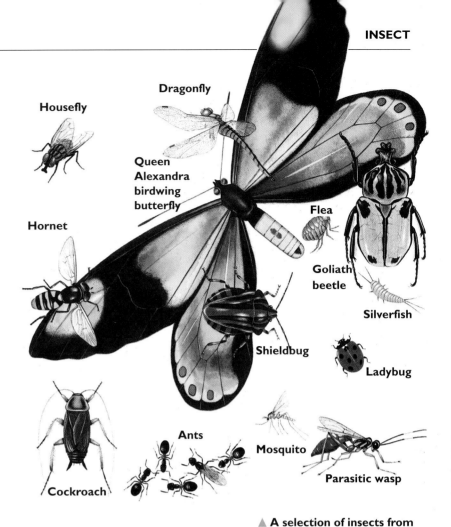

Housefly

Dragonfly

Queen Alexandra birdwing butterfly

Hornet

Flea

Goliath beetle

Silverfish

Shieldbug

Ladybug

Ants

Mosquito

Cockroach

Parasitic wasp

▲ A selection of insects from the wide variety that can be found around the world.

world's food supply. Cattle and other farm animals can be washed or dusted with insecticides to protect them from harmful or annoying flies, ticks, mites, or lice. These farm animals grow larger and are healthier than unprotected animals. Insecticides can control deadly diseases, such as typhus and malaria, by spraying the breeding places of insects that spread these diseases.

The world today depends on insecticides to protect crops and animals and to help people avoid many serious diseases. But insecticides can cause many serious problems, too, and they must be used carefully and wisely. For example, DDT, which used to be widely used as a spray for crops, found its way into the water supply, affecting fish and other animals. Because of its harmful effects, the use of DDT was banned almost entirely by the U.S. government in 1972. Other insecticides kill useful insects at the same time as they kill harmful insects or pests.

The flea is the champion jumper of the animal world. It can jump 100 times its own height and do a broad jump 200 times its own length. This is like a human being jumping more than 500 feet (150 m) into the air and achieving a long jump of more than 1,000 feet (300 m).

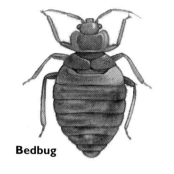

Bedbug

Flea

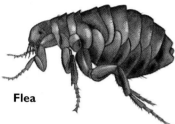

Louse

▶ The parts of an insect showing the three very distinct sections of its body: head, thorax, and abdomen.

▼ When wasps and bees emerge from their eggs, they are already fully formed. Moths have to go through a caterpillar stage first.

Eight-spotted forester moth and caterpillar

Paper wasp

◀ Three insects that feed on people. The bedbug hides by day and sucks blood at night. The human flea can jump many times its own height to reach its prey. It also sucks blood, as does the human louse.

Helpful Insects

Many insects are helpful to people. Some are important pollen carriers. Bees, wasps, moths, and other insects that feed on nectar carry pollen from one flower to another, pollinating the flowers. The pollinated flowers eventually become fruits.

Some insects produce materials useful to people. Bees make honey and wax. Silkworms make silk.

Among the most helpful insects are those that prey on insect pests. Ladybug beetles eat great numbers of aphids, which are harmful to food and flower crops. Several kinds of wasps lay their eggs in caterpillars that eat food crops. The wasp larvae that hatch from the eggs eat the caterpillars. Certain flies, called tachinas, destroy squash bugs, mealy bugs, gypsy-moth larvae, and other harmful insects. Praying mantises eat grasshoppers, and dragonflies eat mosquitoes.

The Structure of Insects

Although there are many different kinds of insects, all of them have bodies that set them apart from other kinds of animals. Every insect's body is divided into three main parts: a head, a thorax, and an abdomen. And every insect has three pairs of jointed legs. The head of an insect is,

of course, at the front, the thorax is in the middle, and the abdomen is at the rear.

On an insect's head is a pair of antennae, which are for touch, taste, and smell. Every insect also has a pair of compound eyes, usually one on each side of the head. Each compound eye is made up of thousands of tiny lenses. Most adult insects also have three simple eyes that form a triangle on the forehead. The mouth parts of insects are either jaws used for chewing, or tubes used for piercing and sucking. A grasshopper has jaws, a housefly has a sucking tube, a horsefly has a rasping tongue and a sucking tube, and a mosquito has a tube for piercing and sucking.

An insect's six legs are attached to the thorax in three pairs. Each leg has five parts connected by joints. In some insects, the legs may look different and have different purposes. The front legs of a praying mantis are spiny and strong for grasping prey. The rear legs of a grasshopper are very long and strong for jumping.

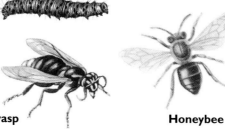

Honeybee

Thorax — Wings — Abdomen — Head — Compound eye — Legs — Antenna

Many insects have two pairs of wings, which are attached to the thorax. In some insects, such as beetles and grasshoppers, the front pair is thick and tough, and serves as a cover that protects the other pair. A beetle's heavy front wings protect most of its body, too. An insect's wings may be transparent, as in dragonflies, or covered with brightly colored scales, as in moths and butterflies. Some insects' wings carry them long distances. Others are used only for short, quick flights from danger. Some insects have no wings at all.

An insect's abdomen is made up of ten *segments,* or sections. The abdomen contains food-digesting and reproductive organs.

The outer part of an insect's body is made up of a tough material called *chitin*. This is the insect's skeleton. It protects the insect's inner organs.

A knot of nerve tissues serving as a kind of brain is located in an insect's head. From this brain, pairs of nerves run the length of the body, connecting smaller knots of nerves called *ganglia*. From the ganglia, nerves go to, and return from, the organs.

Along both sides of an insect's body are rows of openings, called *spiracles*, through which an insect breathes. Air entering a spiracle goes through a tube called a *trachea*. This tube divides into smaller and smaller branches that carry air to inner parts of the insect's body. In insects, blood does not carry oxygen. However, insect blood does carry food substances and *hormones* (special chemicals).

Many kinds of insects have developed special organs. Insects that make sounds—grasshoppers (including katydids) and crickets—have organs of hearing. These are located either on the front legs or in the first segment of the abdomen. Some moths, too, have organs of hearing. Insects have short hairs that are organs of touch, especially around the mouth. Other insects have special glands that produce poisons. And some insects have special organs, such as stingers, for defense or attack.

Reproduction and Growth

A female insect has organs called *ovaries* that form and store eggs. At the rear of the abdomen is a tube called an *ovipositor*, through which the female lays the eggs. Some insects, such as queen termites, lay hundreds of thousands of eggs. A male insect has *testes*, organs that produce *sperm* (male sex cells). It also has an organ to deposit the sperm into the female.

All insects hatch from eggs. Some look much like adults when they hatch. Newly hatched grasshoppers look like "grownups," except they have no wings or sex organs. These young insects are called *nymphs*. Periodically the nymph sheds its skeleton, grows larger, and forms a new, larger skeleton. This process, which is controlled by hormones produced by the nymph, is called *molting*. A nymph usually goes through at least four to six molts before becoming an adult. The process of a young insect gradually changing into an adult is called *incomplete metamorphosis*. Each successive stage is more like the adult insect.

Many kinds of insects go through major changes in body form on their way to becoming adults. In this process, a wormlike creature called a *larva* hatches from the egg. The larva feeds and grows for a period lasting from a day or two to many months. When fully grown, the larva produces a liquid that hardens when it comes into contact with air. The larva completely covers itself with the liquid. The hardened covering is called a *pupa case*; the insect inside is a *pupa*.

The pupa undergoes great changes and finally breaks out of the pupa case as a fully developed insect, called an *imago*. This process of growth in four main steps—egg, larva, pupa, and imago—is called *complete metamorphosis*. Moths, butterflies, mosquitoes, and flies are some insects that go through complete metamorphosis.

▶▶▶▶ FIND OUT MORE ◀◀◀◀

Animal; Animal Kingdom; Ant; Bee; Butterflies and Moths; Dragonfly; Fly; Gland; Hormone; Louse; Metamorphosis; Mosquito; Parasite; Wasps and Hornets

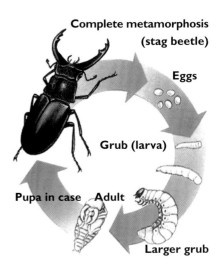

Complete metamorphosis (stag beetle)

Eggs

Grub (larva)

Larger grub

Adult

Pupa in case

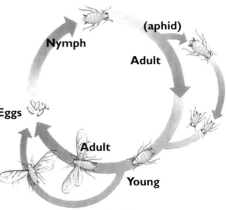

Incomplete metamorphosis (aphid)

Nymph

Adult

Eggs

Adult

Young

Winged adults mate

▲ **When an animal or an insect changes its appearance as it grows, it is known as metamorphosis.**

QUIZ

1. What is the name for a young insect?
2. In what year was the insecticide DDT banned in the U.S.? Why?
3. What are the three parts of an insect's body?
4. How do insects breathe?
5. Are spiders insects?

(Answers on page 1408)

INSECT-EATING PLANT

Pitcher plant

Venus's-flytrap

Insects destroy many, many plants each year. You have probably seen many trees, flowers, bushes, and vegetables spoiled by insects. But what is surprising is that some plants "fight back" by eating insects. The plants trap the insects and then digest them. Insects are not the only food of these plants. Like other green plants, their leaves produce starch, which the plants use as food. Insect-eating plants live in wet places, where the soil lacks nitrogen, which is important to plant growth. These plants get nitrogen from the insects' bodies.

The largest insect-eating plant is the *pitcher plant*. The leaves of this plant form a pitcher-shaped container that holds rainwater. The rim of the pitcher has scales or stiff hairs pointing downward. Insects that enter the "pitcher" are unable to climb out because of the hairs or scales. In their struggle, the insects fall into the water and drown. They are then digested by the plant.

The *sundew* has leaves covered with sticky tentacles. When an insect lands on the leaf, the tentacles bend toward the insect and trap it, and secrete an acid that digests the insect.

The *Venus's-flytrap* has leaves folded in the middle, so that each leaf looks like a clamshell. Around the edges of each leaf are toothlike spikes, and on the surface of each half of the leaf are sensitive bristles. When an insect touches one of these bristles, the halves close suddenly, like a mouth snapping shut. The spikes form a cage that traps the insect. Venus's-flytraps catch mostly crawling insects, because most flying insects are quick enough to take flight and escape.

The *bladderwort* is a water plant that has many one-eighth-inch-long (3-mm) bladders, each with a trap-door equipped with sensitive bristles. When an insect touches a bristle, the trapdoor swings inward with a rush of water that sweeps the insect into the bladder.

▲ **Plants such as the Venus's-flytrap and the pitcher plant trap insects to make up for the poor soil in which they grow.**

▶ ▶ ▶ ▶ **FIND OUT MORE** ◀ ◀ ◀ ◀
Flower; Plant

INSULATION

A ski jacket keeps you warm in winter. It *insulates* your body and prevents heat from escaping into the cold air. Mammals that live in cold climates grow thick coats to protect them from cold weather. Woolen and fur clothing insulates people from the cold. The air trapped in fur or wool provides excellent insulation. The word *insulation* comes from the Latin *insula*, which means "island." Insulation surrounds an object and prevents the passage of not only heat, but also of electricity and sound.

Asbestos, cotton, wool, rubber,

LEARN BY DOING

To see how insulation works, find a large cardboard carton and two smaller boxes, such as detergent or cereal boxes, and remove the tops. You will also need a small table lamp with a 40- or 60-watt bulb, two thermometers, and shredded paper.

Stuff one of the smaller boxes with the paper, placing one thermometer in its center. Place the other thermometer into the other small box, which has no paper stuffing. Now put both boxes into the carton with the lighted lamp between them.

Leave the lamp on for half an hour, then check the thermometers. What has happened? If you extend the time to one hour, what will happen? Can you explain this method of insulation?

Shredded paper

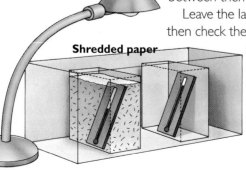

and wood are good *insulators*. Glass and porcelain also insulate. Metals are very poor insulators but are very good *conductors* (substances that carry heat, electricity, or sound).

A house must be insulated to keep heat in during cold weather and out during hot weather. Thick stone or brick walls are good for this purpose. Wooden frame houses must have both outside walls and inside walls. The space between these walls provides some insulation, but it is better to fill this space with an insulating material such as rock wool or fiberglass. The roof of a house must be well insulated to keep hot air, which rises, from escaping through the top of the house in cold weather. Roof insulation also keeps the summer sun from heating the house up.

Metal wires, which are good conductors, are used to carry electricity. To keep people from getting a severe shock, the wires are insulated with a covering of rubber, plastic, or tightly woven cotton fabric.

A home or apartment is insulated for sound in much the same way as it is for heat. Single walls must be thick enough, and double walls must have enough space between them, to keep sound out. Many people who live in thin-walled apartments can hear sounds from the next apartment. Sound insulation is also used to keep sounds from becoming too loud and too confusing. Theaters, concert halls, restaurants, and other large rooms have special coverings on their walls and ceilings. These coverings, such as fiberboard, absorb much of the sound, whereas sound bounces off stone and plaster walls. Curtains and draperies are also effective in absorbing sound and reducing noise.

▶▶▶▶ **FIND OUT MORE** ◀◀◀◀
Electricity; Heat and Cold; Sound

INSULIN

SEE BANTING, FREDERICK; DRUG

INSURANCE

An accident can cause severe injury to people and costly damage to property. Safety measures are the best protection against accidents. But when accidents do happen, having insurance can protect you.

Insurance is a kind of protection sold by insurance companies. It is based on the fact that a lot of people share the risks (and costs) of losses. For example, a person wishing to buy automobile insurance will pay a certain amount of money, or *premium*, to an insurance company. In return, the insurance company will issue a *policy*, or contract, to the individual. The company agrees to pay for all or part of the losses or damages to, or caused by, that person's car. At the same time, thousands of other people are also paying the company for the same kind of insurance. Most of these people will never have an accident, so the insurance company will never have to pay them money for any damages or losses. But the money that these thousands of people have paid to the company is usually enough to cover the losses or damages that some of them will have.

What do insurance companies do with the extra money? Some of the money is kept for a constant supply of cash. Some of the money is used for operating expenses—salaries, rent, supplies. And some is invested for profit.

The *premium rate*, or cost of insurance, is based upon averages. This means that the company will figure out how many times something happens, or is likely to happen, during a given time in a certain place.

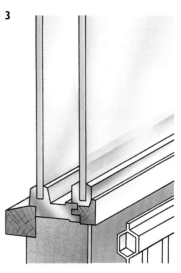

▲ **Many types of insulation are used in houses to reduce heat loss. 1. Fiberglass is used to line roof spaces; 2. Foam can be pumped into wall cavities; and 3. Windows can be double-glazed.**

◀ **Rubber is a very effective natural insulator and is still used with electric cable.**

It is estimated that the average household in the United States pays more than $1,500 a year in insurance premiums.

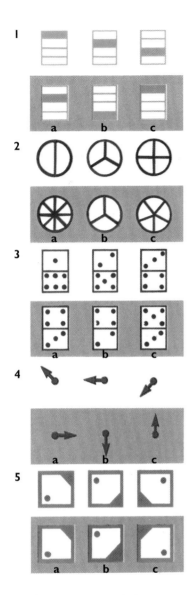

▲ One characteristic of intelligence is the ability to detect patterns. The first three pictures in each set follow a pattern. Choose one picture from the three pictures under each set to complete the patterns.
(Answers on page 1408)

Of all the nations that have produced figures for their national IQ, Japan comes first with a figure of 111. It is believed that more than one-tenth of the Japanese people have IQs greater than 125.

Then the company decides what chance the policyholder has of being involved in such an event. For example, an automobile owner living in a big city will be more likely to have an accident than one who lives in a small town, where traffic is lighter. So the automobile insurance usually costs more in and around big cities.

People can buy many other kinds of insurance. Many musicians are insured in case anything happens to injure their hands. People who plan to vacation in a sunny place can be insured against rain that could spoil their vacation. People—especially those with families or those who support a family—can buy life insurance so that when they die, the company will pay money to the *next of kin* (closest relative) or to their family. Fire insurance is bought so that if a house or apartment is damaged or destroyed by fire, the owner will have enough money to replace any losses. A homeowner's insurance policy may also include protection of such valuable items as cameras, stereos, jewelry, and silver. Health insurance helps to pay doctors' bills and hospital bills. Many farmers also buy insurance against crop losses caused by nature, such as earthquakes and floods.

Many people buy life, health, and homeowner's insurance, as well as automobile insurance. In most states, automobile insurance is *mandatory* (must be bought). Liability insurance is often included in automobile policies. This means that if a driver has an accident in which a person is injured, the driver's insurance covers the medical bills of the injured person. If a driver is sued, liability insurance is used to pay the lawsuit.

Perhaps the most famous insurers in the world are Lloyds of London. This company is reputed to insure anything from racehorses to supertankers and space rockets.

Hartford, Connecticut is known as the insurance capital of the world. A number of major insurance companies have their headquarters there. More insurance business is carried out in Hartford than anywhere else in the world.

▶▶▶▶ **FIND OUT MORE** ◀◀◀◀
Chance and Probability; Statistics

INTEGRATION

SEE CIVIL RIGHTS MOVEMENT; BLACK AMERICANS

⚙ INTELLIGENCE

Scientists define intelligence as the ability to learn or to understand. People who are intelligent learn what they are taught easily and quickly. Intelligent people also remember what they have learned. This knowledge can then be used in new situations or

▲ Intelligence can be defined as the ability to learn and to understand. At 9 months of age an infant has learned to grip. Many old people are wise because of their many years of experience.

problems. When intelligent people are faced with some problem or situation that they have never met before, they will use their knowledge and memory of situations in the past to solve the problem.

Many psychologists believe that intelligence can be measured with various kinds of tests. These scientists believe that if a person can deal intelligently with some problem in a test, he or she will also deal intelligently with problems in everyday life.

Psychologists express the results of an intelligence test in a number called an IQ (*intelligence quotient*). To determine this number, they first give tests to find the person's mental age. Two young people of 8 and 16 may both have a mental age of 12. The younger person has obviously developed further than the older. But their mental age does not show the difference in their degree of mental growth. The mental age of the younger person is far above his or her *chronological age* (age in years). But the older person's mental age is far below his or her chronological age. Therefore, psychologists developed the formula below.

$$IQ = \frac{MA \text{ (mental age)} \times 100}{CA \text{ (chronological age)}}$$

This means that the person's mental age is divided by his or her chronological age. The quotient is multiplied by 100, and the number that results is the IQ. This number represents the way that someone's intelligence compares with that of other people of his or her age. The 8-year-old person's IQ is 150; the 16-year-old's IQ is 75.

But many people believe that intelligence tests do not really measure someone's ability. Many tests seem to measure *what* someone has learned rather than how quickly or well he or she can learn. Other people think that intelligence cannot be measured accurately.

What makes one person intelligent and another not so intelligent? Are people born with the basic intelligence that they will have all their lives? Is intelligence affected by a person's home life or the number of books he or she reads? Scientists are still studying these questions.

Human beings are the most intelligent animals. People have built cities, written books, and traveled to the moon. Since a human being is certainly not the biggest animal, or the animal with the biggest brain, intelligence cannot be measured by size. But studies of other animals are showing

that a human being is definitely not the *only* animal with intelligence.

Other animals can communicate with each other, but they cannot read. They cannot do mathematics or build complicated things like automobiles or airplanes. Still, animals learn very quickly the things they have to know in order to stay alive and healthy. Animals also remember things they have learned.

An animal in the jungle knows who its enemies are, and it keeps out of their way. It knows what foods are good for it and how to find these foods. Animals teach these things to their young.

Many people believe that animals are not intelligent at all. These people say that animals have *instincts*, not intelligence. An *instinctive* act is something done automatically without having to learn it. For example, a newborn baby knows automatically

The highest tested IQ was achieved by Marilyn Mach vos Savant of St. Louis, Missouri. As a child of 10, she scored a record IQ of 230.

▲ **Young chimpanzees learn to dig out termites from dirt mounds by watching their mothers do it. Intelligent animals learn by copying their parents.**

▲ Guide dogs have been trained as the "eyes" of their blind or partially sighted human owners. The dogs' ability to learn skills such as this has proved to be very important to humans.

Until the 1500s, most people opposed the charging of interest on loans. In fact, they thought that charging interest for any reason was wrong. Lending money was considered to be a duty that the rich owed the poor.

how to suck milk from a bottle or its mother's breast. No one has to teach the baby how to suck milk. Sucking is an instinct.

Monkeys in the jungle live together in large groups. Sometimes there are hundreds of monkeys living together. Yet, each baby monkey knows its own mother. The mothers can always tell their own babies from the other babies.

Some animals act in very intelligent ways. Dolphins even have a language. They can "talk" to each other by making whistling and clicking sounds. If a dolphin is in danger, it can call other dolphins to help it. Dolphins can even work together and get a complicated job done that one dolphin alone could not do. They often work together without seeing each other. They talk to each other in their language over long distances and coordinate a "plan."

Many animals can be trained to do things that they do not usually do. Dogs can be trained to do tricks and to perform useful tasks such as leading blind people or herding sheep. Lions, tigers, seals, bears, and chimpanzees may be trained to perform in circuses. Rats use intelligence to get at food that seems out of their reach. They also learn to avoid food that has been poisoned.

▶▶▶▶ FIND OUT MORE ◀◀◀◀
Learning; Memory

INTEREST

If a person borrows money, he or she expects to pay for the use of it. The amount the person borrowed is paid back, along with an additional amount called *interest*. In the same way, a company may sell stocks or bonds to investors to raise money, and pay interest on the shares to compensate the investors.

The amount of interest is calculated as a percentage—that is, so many dol-

lars for every hundred dollars loaned or invested. If a borrower is paying 8 percent, he pays $8 every year for the use of every $100 borrowed.

Simple interest is just a straight annual payment. *Compound interest* is the result of adding the interest to the sum borrowed. In the above example, at the end of the first year the $8 would be added to the $100 borrowed, so the second year's interest would be paid on $108, and would be $8.64.

▶▶▶▶ FIND OUT MORE ◀◀◀◀
Stocks and Bonds

INTERIOR DECORATING

Interior decorating is the art of making rooms attractive, comfortable, and useful. It involves selecting decorations and planning the design of rooms.

People who earn a living doing this are called *interior designers* or *interior decorators*. They are trained in the use of space, color, light, fabrics, and furniture. Most people, however, do their own interior decorating. They learn about decorating by looking at different styles of furniture in stores and in other people's homes. Decorating magazines also give many good ideas.

History
No one knows when people first thought of making their homes beautiful. In ancient Egypt, Greece, and Rome, the upper classes had colorfully decorated homes. The ancient Romans carefully planned their rooms according to how these rooms were used. They used great artistic skill in making furniture and room decorations.

After the Roman Empire fell, interior decoration became unimportant in Europe. Furniture was simple— usually just stools, tables, and storage boxes. Europeans traveling to the

Middle East during the Crusades discovered the beautiful decorations and carved furniture of the Orient. Trade routes with the Middle East were set up. By the 1400s, wealthy Europeans were buying Oriental furniture and copying Oriental designs. Ruling families became *patrons* of decorators. They supported the decorators in exchange for having rooms beautifully furnished. Walls were hung with velvet draperies, mirrors, tapestries, and handmade wallpaper. Some furniture was *gilded* (covered with gold) or beautifully carved.

During the 1600s and 1700s, the wealthy people of France introduced decorated plaster ceilings, delicate fabrics, and huge glass chandeliers that held many candles. The French used brass and tortoiseshell for their furniture, which was light and graceful. As trade with the Orient expanded, styles of decoration from China and Japan became popular.

American styles of furnishing were based on those of Europe. The earliest style is now called Early American and is still popular, as is the Federal style of the early 1800s.

After the Industrial Revolution, furniture could be factory-made at lower prices. Many people could then afford to have at least some beautiful pieces in their homes.

Techniques of Interior Design

Planning is an important part of interior decorating. The designer must first list the activities that take place in each room. Will the living room be used to entertain friends? Will people read and relax there? Will people gather together in the living room to watch television? The answers to these and other questions will help the designer decide how to arrange the room. If the room is used for entertaining, comfortable chairs should be arranged so that people can talk together easily. If the room is used for reading, it will need good lighting. If people will be watching television in the living room, the television must be placed so that everyone will be able to see it.

The designer must also study the shape of the room. How long is it and how wide? How many windows and doors does it have? What is the easiest way for people to pass through the room? (This is called the *traffic pattern*.) These things help the designer decide where to put the furniture.

The designer must think about the floor, too. Is it made of hard polished wood, linoleum, or tiles? Wood floors are attractive, but walking on them can be noisy. If the room is in an apartment with people living below, rugs or carpeting will probably be needed to lessen the noise.

When the designer has studied the room and how it is used, he or she then decides what colors will be used in it. The choice of color is important because colors are connected with

◀ **In ancient Rome, the rich decorated the floors and walls of their homes with beautiful mosaics made from thousands of tiny pieces of colored stone.**

Until the 1500s, rich people decorated the walls of their rooms with tapestry, velvets, and damasks. Then it was discovered that a much cheaper and quite pleasing effect could be had by covering the walls with sheets of paper made for the linings of books. The designs on this "wallpaper" were probably checkered or marbled and the sheets were only about 12 by 16 inches (30 by 40 cm). They were nailed to the walls.

▼ **A traditional Japanese interior is characterized by low furniture, matting on the floor, and cushions in place of chairs. The design is simple and harmonious.**

▲ **This stained-glass lamp by Louis Tiffany belongs to the decorative style called Art Nouveau, which was popular at the end of the 1800s.**

▼ **The world's time zones. There is one hour's time difference for every 15 degrees of longitude.**

moods or feelings. Reds and oranges usually have a warm feeling, while blues and bluegreens have a cool feeling. Bright colors often put people in a happy mood, while dark, dull colors put them in a sad mood. Also, light colors make rooms seem larger, and dark colors make them seem smaller. The designer must consider all these things when choosing a *color scheme*.

Color schemes can be a combination of blending colors or contrasting colors. *Blending colors* are those that are similar, such as yellow and orange. *Contrasting colors* are those that are quite different from each other.

A designer picks furniture that fits the activities and tastes of the people who use the room. Many people like *contemporary,* or modern furniture, which has plain, undecorated lines and can be made of wood, metal, fabric, or plastic. Other people feel more comfortable with *traditional* furniture modeled after furniture styles of the past. Traditional furniture is usually made of wood and

fabric only. Designers will often combine different styles of furniture in one room.

Accessories are the ornaments used in a room to give it "personality." They include lamps, cushions, vases, pieces of pottery, and pictures. Accessories also include things such as plants, a display of a collection, or other special objects. Such accessories in a room tell something about the people who live there.

▶▶▶▶ **FIND OUT MORE** ◀◀◀◀
Antique; Carpets and Rugs; Color;
Furniture; House; Lighting

 ## INTERNATIONAL DATE LINE

If you look at a map of the world or a globe, you will see lines that extend north and south between the poles. These are the lines of *longitude*. They are also called *meridians*. The globe is divided into 360 *degrees*, or parts. Each degree of longitude represents $\frac{1}{360}$ of the distance around the globe.

International Date Line   **Greenwich Meridian**

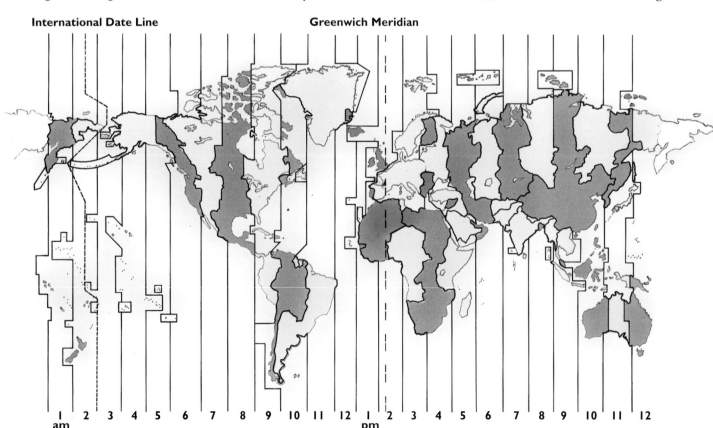

| 1 | 2 | 3 | 4 | 5 | 6 | 7 | 8 | 9 | 10 | 11 | 12 | 1 | 2 | 3 | 4 | 5 | 6 | 7 | 8 | 9 | 10 | 11 | 12 |
am   pm

These imaginary lines make it possible to tell the location of a place east or west from the *prime meridian*. The prime meridian, which runs through Greenwich, England, is regarded as zero degrees. Every place in the world is located a certain number of degrees east or west of the prime meridian.

Starting from any place on Earth and moving in a straight line east or west, you must cross 360 degrees of longitude to get back to where you started. As the Earth rotates, the path of the sun seems to move from east to west. This means that the sun seems to move 15 degrees west every hour. When it is noon in England, it is five hours before noon (7 A.M.) on the east coast of the United States. When it is noon on the east coast of the United States, it is three hours before noon (9 A.M.) on the west coast.

But where does the date change? The nations of the world have agreed that the date changes at 180 degrees longitude, the 180th meridian. This imaginary line is called the *International Date Line*. It runs from pole to pole, mostly through the Pacific Ocean. The Date Line does not follow the 180th meridian exactly. It bends to the east to include Siberia with Russia. Then it bends to the west to include the Aleutian Islands with Alaska. It bends to the east to keep all the Fiji Islands together.

Each date begins on the west side of the Date Line and ends on the east side. If you could stand just east of the line and your friends could stand just west of it, they would be one whole day (24 hours) ahead of you. You could watch them open their presents and eat Christmas dinner— but for you, it would still be Christmas Eve. And as they watched you open your presents and eat Christmas dinner, their calendar would tell them it was December 26!

▶ ▶ ▶ ▶ **FIND OUT MORE** ◀ ◀ ◀ ◀
Latitude and Longitude; Map; Time

🌐 INTERNATIONAL LAW

Nations, like people, are guided by certain customs and rules. The rules that guide the way nations behave to each other are known as *international law*.

The idea of international law was developed in the 1600s by the Dutch statesman, Hugo Grotius. Grotius described certain rules that he thought all nations should obey. These rules would be based on custom—the way nations usually act. They would also be based on treaties—written agreements signed by two or more nations.

In the 1800s and early 1900s, the major Western nations of the world met together and agreed upon a system of international law. For example, these laws state that in peacetime every nation has a right to govern its own territory and to control its ambassadors and embassies abroad. A nation must declare war before attacking another nation. Soldiers wounded in war must be given medical care. Warring armies must not pass through the land of a *neutral* nation, one that favors neither side in a war.

If nations do not obey international laws, as often happens in times of war, they may be urged to do so by an international organization, the United Nations. *Sanctions* (penalties for disobedience) may be applied against the offending country. For example, other countries may be forbidden to trade with that country. The International Court of Justice, which was set up by the United Nations, also helps to settle international disputes by the rules of international law. The UN Security Council may also agree to use force to stop aggression.

▶ ▶ ▶ ▶ **FIND OUT MORE** ◀ ◀ ◀ ◀
International Relations; League of Nations; Treaty; United Nations; War

The continental United States has four time zones: Eastern, Central, Mountain, and Pacific. These zones are 5,6,7, and 8 hours, respectively, behind Greenwich Mean Time.

▼ A Norwegian soldier, part of a U.N. peacekeeping force in Lebanon. Forces such as these act like policemen, trying to stop fighting in troubled areas.

INTERNATIONAL RELATIONS

Relations among nations are a bit like those among members of a family. Most family members want to get along with each other. Most nations want to get along with other nations. Family members want to feel secure in their home. Nations want to feel secure also. No nation wants to live in fear of attack by another country. Each wants to govern itself as it wishes, without interference.

The guiding factor in family relationships is usually love. Members of a family are concerned about one another and help one another because they love each other. The guiding factor in international relations is usually *self-interest*. Nations help each other if doing so will benefit them in some way. Each nation looks out for itself.

How Does Self-Interest Work?

A nation may protect its own interests in several ways. The most obvious way is to build a large, well-trained army, with modern weapons. Even if the army never goes into battle, its very existence keeps other nations from interfering in that country's affairs or invading its land. Some nations have gained a lot for themselves by international trade. If a country has a much-needed product,

such as oil, or if its industry is very strong, it can make agreements to supply other nations with products that they need. This increases a country's income. The strong trading nation can stop supplying needed products (or threaten to stop supplying them) in order to get what it wants from other nations. A nation that buys a great deal from one country can threaten to start buying from some other country if the nation from whom it buys begins to interfere.

Probably the best place to see self-interest at work is in international negotiations. Nations discuss their differences and try to reach an agreement that is acceptable to all of them. Each nation first states its position. It tells the other what it wants. As negotiations progress, each nation sees that it cannot have everything it wants. Each must *concede* (give up) some things in order to agree on other things. Each nation tries to concede only the less important things. Each nation looks out for its own self-interest, trying to get as much out of the negotiations as possible, but conceding as little as possible.

Economics

Every nation wants wealth. Wealth creates a better standard of living and it brings power. The search for wealth often brings nations into contact with one another. In earlier times, this search led some nations to establish colonies in other lands. These colonies provided raw materials for the industries of the colonizing nation and markets for its goods. Throughout history, countries have increased their wealth by trading with one another. Today, nations in the same geographic area form associations to increase their economic or political power. One of these is the European Community, or Common Market.

History

International relations have been conducted in many ways. In ancient

▲ This American cartoon eloquently expressed how the United States regarded Britain during the War of 1812. Here, Britain, depicted as John Bull, is being "stung" with defeats by the U.S. navy.

▼ Heads of government of the seven major industrial democratic nations (Group of 7) meet to discuss the world's economy.

times, strong nations such as Rome conquered territories and built great empires. During the Middle Ages and the Renaissance, most of western Europe was made up of small territories ruled by princes. These rulers were continually struggling for power among themselves. European nations, as we know them, began to be formed in the 1300s. They were based on the idea of *national sovereignty*. This meant that each nation was independent and had the right to govern itself.

Nations tried to keep peace by preventing any one nation from being so powerful that it threatened the other nations. This system is called a *balance of power*. When one nation showed signs of becoming too powerful, others would form an *alliance* against it. They agreed to help one another in case of political interference, military attack, or even for economic reasons. An alliance on one side often led to a *counteralliance* on the other. Each side tried to become stronger than the other. In the 1800s, Great Britain kept a balance of power in Europe by allying itself first with one side, then with the other.

A new power balance, called the *Cold War*, lasted for more than 40 years after World War II. The United States and western European nations stood on one side; the Soviet Union, its Communist allies in eastern Europe, and the People's Republic of China on the other. The fall of Communism in eastern Europe and the collapse of the Soviet Union ended the Cold War. Russia and other parts of the former Soviet Union are adjusting to democracy. Some eastern European countries now wish to join the European Community.

International relations today have been influenced by the United Nations. The United Nations serves as a meetingplace where countries can argue about their disagreements and sometimes find solutions that may prevent their going to war. The

United Nations also tries to persuade countries to obey international law in their relations with one another.

Official relations among nations are carried on by *ambassadors* and their staffs of foreign service officers. An ambassador is an official representative of his or her government in a foreign country. Ambassadors must keep informed of the policies and decisions of their country's government. They must also be good at persuading the foreign government to agree with, or at least understand, their country's policies. Ambassadors must advise their government on how to deal with the policies and actions of the foreign country. Relations between countries are some-

▲ **This nineteenth century cartoon shows Germany and Austria-Hungary making many protective treaties with other European nations in an attempt to isolate France. Political cartoons like this one became popular in the early 1800s.**

▼ **The United Nations General Assembly. The auditorium is large enough to allow representatives from all member countries to take part in debates. Each country has one equal vote.**

times carried out by heads of government, as when the President of the United States meets with the leaders of other nations.

▼ **When fully loaded, a modern multicargo ship makes maximum use of its capacity.**

►►►► FIND OUT MORE ◄◄◄◄
International Alliances see Commonwealth of Independent States; Commonwealth of Nations; European Community; North Atlantic Treaty Organization; Organization of American States; Warsaw Pact
International Diplomacy see Foreign Service
International Organizations see League of Nations; United Nations
International Relations and Economics see Colony; Economics; International Trade; Nation
Relations between Countries see International Law; Treaty; War

INTERNATIONAL TRADE

Every country engages in international trade. A country sells some things that it produces to other countries. Products sent out of the country are called *exports*. A country also buys products that it needs from other countries. Products brought into the country are called *imports*. International trade takes place because countries generally produce more of certain things than they need, and not enough of other things that they want. For example, Japan is a leading manufacturer of automobiles. It exports cars and other goods to other nations. But Japan cannot raise enough food to feed its population, so it imports food from nations that raise great amounts of agricultural products.

Why do nations produce large amounts of some products and not enough of others? Nature is one reason. Oranges, for instance, grow best in hot climates. Some metals, such as copper, are found only in certain areas of the world. Each nation concentrates on the products it can produce

at home, or that it can produce at a lower cost than the import price.

Every country needs to trade. Sometimes other nations will impose trading "sanctions" on a country. They will stop trading with them in order to put pressure on them. For example, when Saddam Hussein invaded Kuwait in 1990, the United Nations stopped trading with Iraq.

All nations try to keep a good *balance of payments*. This is the comparison between money coming into a country when it sells exports, and the amount of money going out when a country buys imports. When a country exports more than it imports, more money comes into the country than goes out of it. This is considered a favorable balance of payments.

Governments sometimes set up *tariffs* (taxes on imports) or *quotas* (limits on the amount of goods that may be imported). Tariffs and quotas raise the prices of products coming into a country. The higher the prices on products, the less trade takes place. People will not buy most imports if they cost more than the products made in their own country. Tariffs and quotas are usually set up by a government to protect the farmers and manufacturers of its own country. For example, if the United States puts a tariff on imported cars, these become more expensive than U.S. cars, so people are more likely to buy the cheaper American cars.

Some nations have formed "trading communities" to avoid these tariffs, and to promote free trade among the member nations. The European Community is a trading community in western Europe, and in 1992 it gained closer economic unity. Soon all the nations may have the same currency. Members of the Commonwealth of Nations also have trade agreements.

►►►► FIND OUT MORE ◄◄◄◄
European Community; Commonwealth of Nations

U.S. TRADING PARTNERS
($ billion: 1991)

Exporters to U.S.
1. Canada (93)
2. Japan (91.5)
3. Mexico (31.5)
4. Germany (26.1)
5. Taiwan (23)

Importers of U.S. Goods
1. Canada (85.1)
2. Japan (47.4)
3. Mexico (33.1)
4. United Kingdom (21.5)
5. Germany (20.7)

⚙ INVENTION

Look around your home or classroom and observe the tools and other objects that you use every day. You will begin to see how much you depend on inventions in your daily life. The books you read in school would not have been possible without the invention of paper and ink—or of printing itself. Pencils, pens, typewriters, staplers, and pencil sharpeners are also useful inventions. Both your school and home have electric lights and heating systems made possible by the work of inventors. At home you may also have a refrigerator, telephone, radio, TV, and other useful things.

▲ The invention of the pulley in about 400 B.C. made it easier to lift heavy loads and was a great aid to building.

Countless other inventions are vital to industry, business, medicine, farming, and other fields.

An invention may be the creation of something completely new or an improvement on something made before. Many important inventions have resulted from the work of one individual. Inventors often owe much to discoveries and inventions made by others before them. For instance, James Watt invented the first workable steam engine, but his invention was based on earlier models built by others. Samuel F. B. Morse's telegraph, however, was a completely original invention.

SOME IMPORTANT INVENTIONS

Year	Invention	Inventor(s)	Nationality
c.1447	Movable type printing	Johannes Gutenberg	German
1592	Thermometer	Galileo Galilei	Italian
1608	Telescope	Hans Lippershey	Dutch
1642	Adding machine	Blaise Pascal	French
1705	Steam engine	Thomas Newcomen	British
1793	Cotton gin	Eli Whitney	American
1800	Electric battery	Alessandro Volta	Italian
1804	Steam locomotive	Richard Trevithick	British
1816-1827	Photography	Joseph Nicéphore Niepce	French
1821	Electric motor	Michael Faraday	British
1837	Telegraph	Samuel F. B. Morse	American
1846	Sewing machine	Elias Howe	American
1852	Elevator	Elisha Otis	American
1867	Typewriter	Christopher Sholes Samuel Soule Carlos Glidden	American
1876	Telephone	Alexander Graham Bell	American
1884	Fountain pen	Lewis E. Waterman	American
1885	Gasoline automobile	Karl Benz, Otto Daimler	German
1888	Kodak camera	George Eastman	American
1893	Motion picture machine	Thomas Edison	American
1895	X-ray machine	Wilhelm Roentgen	German
1896	Wireless telegraph	Guglielmo Marconi	Italian
1903	Airplane (with motor)	Orville & Wilbur Wright	American
1907	Radio vacuum tube	Lee De Forest	American
1923-1928	Television	Vladimir Zworykin John L. Baird Philo T. Farnsworth	American British American
1926	Rocket engine	Robert Goddard	American
1926	Aerosol spray	Eric Rotheim	Norwegian
1928	Jet engine	Frank Whittle	British
1935	Radar	Robert Watson-Watt	British
1935	Nylon	Wallace H. Carothers	American
1938	Xerography	Chester Carlson	American
1939	Helicopter	Igor Sikorsky	American
1942	Atomic reactor	Enrico Fermi	Italian
1944	Digital computer	Howard Aiken	American
1944	Ballpoint pen	Lazlo Biro	Argentine
1947	Polaroid camera	Edwin Land	American
1948	Transistor	John Bardeen William Shockley Walter Brattain	American
1955	Optical fibers	Dr. Narinder Kapary	British
1960	Laser	Charles H. Townes Theodore H. Maiman	American
1969	Artificial heart	Michael DeBakey	American
1979	Compact disc player	Sony; Philips Company	Japanese Dutch
1981	Space Shuttle	NASA	American

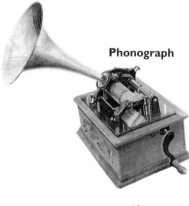

Phonograph

Safety razor

▲ The padded horse collar, originally invented in China, was introduced to Europe in the 1000s. It allowed horses to pull heavy weights without choking themselves.

▼ The phonograph was invented in 1877 by one of America's greatest inventors, Thomas Alva Edison. The invention of the safety razor in 1901, by King Gillette, made clean-shaving fashionable.

At times, two or more inventors, working independently, have come up with the same invention. For example, Elisha Gray and Alexander Graham Bell both applied for a patent on the telephone in 1876. (A *patent* gives an inventor the legal rights to his invention and forbids anyone else to copy it or claim to have invented it.) Later, when he sued Bell to get the patent, Gray couldn't prove that he had invented the telephone, while Bell could. Bell received credit for the invention and kept the patent.

Many modern inventions have been created not by one person, but by many people working together as a team. The atom bomb, for instance, was developed during World War II by a large group of scientists and technicians. Today, research teams in government, industrial, and university laboratories work hard to create new inventions or to improve existing ones.

Not all inventors have been scientists or experts in their fields. Ordinary people have invented useful objects too. Some inventions have even come about by accident. Charles Goodyear, the inventor of vulcanized rubber, was originally a hardware salesman with no formal education. He was trying to find a way to treat natural rubber so that it would not become brittle when cold, or soft and sticky when hot. He made hundreds of unsuccessful experiments, mixing rubber with different materials. Then one day in 1839, Goodyear accidentally dropped some rubber, which he had treated with sulfur, into the fire. The heat gave the mixture the elastic quality he wanted. This method of treating rubber, called *vulcanization*, is still the basis of rubber manufacturing.

The Process of Invention

Many inventions have been brought about by economic, social, or military needs. For example, the invention of the cotton gin by Eli Whitney in 1793 helped agriculture in the South because this machine could remove the seeds from cotton as fast as 50 laborers working by hand could.

◄ Thomas Edison also invented the electric light bulb, the first one of which burned for 40 hours.

Social needs have inspired the development of new medical instruments and drugs in the fight against disease. Roentgen's discovery of X-rays in 1895, for instance, resulted in great advances in the detection and treatment of disease.

Wars have always stimulated invention, both destructive and constructive. The Civil War, for example, produced the Gatling gun, the forerunner of the machine gun. But at the same time, it established the widespread use of the telegraph as a means of fast communication.

History of Inventions

The earliest inventions were tools and weapons that helped people to build shelters and obtain food. Prehistoric people chipped stones with other stones to make simple hammers and axes. They also shaped stones into crude knives and spear points for hunting. These stone tools later gave way to tools made of bronze and iron, as people learned to use metals. Early people also learned to make clothing, first from animal skins and later from plant materials. They invented plows and learned how to plant and harvest grains and other foods. They also dug out logs to make crude boats.

One of the most important early inventions was the wheel. The wheel made carts and wagons possible, as well as inventions such as the potter's wheel and the waterwheel. The waterwheel, believed to have been invented by the Romans about 100 B.C., was a large wheel with paddles attached to the rim. The wheel was put under a waterfall so that the wheel turned when the water struck the paddles. The turning axle of the wheel, attached to a machine, gave the machine power to operate. Waterwheels were used for such jobs as grinding grain and pumping water. Windmills came into use in Europe in the 1100s. Just as the waterwheel used moving water as a source of power, the windmill used the force of air.

Most inventions have been welcomed by society. But some have encountered resistance, especially when new technology has threatened jobs. During the Industrial Revolution, some workers attacked and smashed the new machines that they felt were depriving them of work. Even today, society has to deal with problems arising from new technology. Microchip technology, for example, is reducing the need for people in many factories and offices. And the side effects of inventions such as the automobile, which produces pollution, can be harmful.

▶ ▶ ▶ ▶ **FIND OUT MORE** ◀ ◀ ◀ ◀

Inventions see Air Conditioning; Air Cushion Vehicle; Airplane; Airship; Automobile; Bicycle; Calculator; Camera; Cassette and Cartridges; Clocks and Watches; Compact Disc; Computer; Elevators and Escalators; Explosives; Fiber Optics; Geiger Counter; Guns and Rifles; Gyroscope; Heating; Helicopter; Holography; Hydrofoil; Jet Propulsion; Lasers and Masers; Lens; Lighting; Locks and Keys; Match; Microscope; Motion Picture; Paper; Parachute; Particle Accelerator; Pens and Pencils; Photocopier; Photography; Plastic; Printing; Radar; Radio; Recording; Refrigeration; Rocket; Rubber; Satellite; Scanner, Body; Sewing Machine; Snowmobile; Submarine; Synthetics; Telecommunications; Telegraph; Telephone; Telescope; Television; Thermometer; X-Rays

Inventors see Baird, John L.; Bell, Alexander Graham; Edison, Thomas Alva; Faraday, Michael; Fermi, Enrico; Franklin, Benjamin; Fulton, Robert; Galileo; Goddard, Robert H.; Gutenberg, Johannes; Leonardo Da Vinci; Marconi, Guglielmo; McCormick, Cyrus; Morse, Samuel F.B.; Newton, Sir Isaac; Pascal, Blaise; Stephenson, George; Von Braun, Wernher; Watt, James; Whitney, Eli; Wright Brothers; Zworykin, Vladimir

General see Industrial Revolution; Patents and Copyrights

▲ **The zip fastener, invented in 1891 by an American, Whitcomb L. Judson.**

The United States Patent Office has issued about four million patents for inventions, a number roughly equal to the total issued by the patent offices of Great Britain, Germany, and France combined.

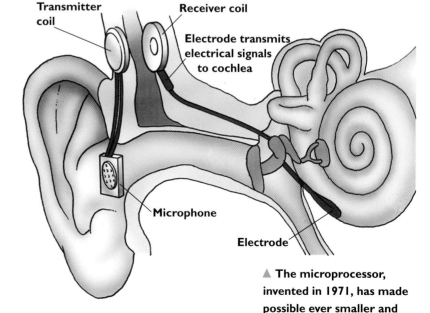

Transmitter coil

Receiver coil

Electrode transmits electrical signals to cochlea

Microphone

Electrode

▲ **The microprocessor, invented in 1971, has made possible ever smaller and more sophisticated technology such as this hearing aid, implanted directly into the ear.**

INVERTEBRATE

SEE ANIMAL KINGDOM

Iowa's first capital was Burlington, but the government moved to Iowa City in 1839, and to Des Moines in 1857.

▲ The Governor's Mansion in Des Moines, Iowa. Built in 1869, it has recently been restored. It was given to the state in 1970.

St. Anthony's Chapel in Festina, Iowa, built in 1885, is said to be the smallest church in the world. It has only four pews.

INVESTMENT

SEE STOCKS AND SHARES

ION

SEE ATOM

IOWA

Iowa reputedly took its name from the Iowa or Ioway Native Americans, one of several tribes that lived in various parts of the state before the white settlers came. The Native Americans liked this prairie region. They raised vegetables in the rich soil and hunted great herds of buffalo on the plains.

The Land and Climate

Iowa lies in the plains that curve west and south of the Great Lakes. Minnesota is north of its straight northern boundary. Missouri is south of its almost-straight southern boundary. Its western boundary line is not straight at all. It is formed by the Missouri River and the Big Sioux River, which flows into the Missouri. Nebraska and South Dakota are Iowa's western neighbors. Its eastern boundary is wavy, too. It is formed by the Mississippi River, which separates Iowa from Illinois and Wisconsin.

Most of Iowa is gently rolling plain. The state is highest in the northwest. It is lowest in the southeast. But it really slopes in *two* directions. The rivers show that it does. The Des Moines River and the other rivers in the eastern two-thirds of Iowa flow southeast toward the Mississippi. The rivers in the western third of the state flow southwest.

Iowa is wonderful farming country. No other state has so much top-grade soil. Most of the Iowa region was covered with tall prairie grass for hundreds of years. The long grass roots added to the plant food in the

soil as they decayed. Iowa also has a very good climate for crops. There is usually enough rain for the crops during the six warm months. It is brought by the winds from the south. The hot sunshine of long summer days helps the crops ripen. Winter winds from the north give Iowa bright days and frosty nights.

History

Prehistoric Native Americans called Mound Builders once lived in Iowa. They built large mounds of earth as burial places or as bases for houses and temples. Most of their mounds are cone-shaped. But some, called *effigy* mounds, are in the form of huge birds or beasts. These interesting mounds can be seen in Effigy Mounds National Monument, near the town of Marquette on the Mississippi River.

The mounds were already old when the first white people arrived. Two French explorers, Louis Joliet and Father Jaques Marquette, came down the Mississippi River in canoes and landed on the Iowa shore on June 25, 1673. La Salle, another French explorer, later traveled down the Mississippi and claimed the entire area drained by the river for France.

Several Native American tribes played important parts in the history of this region. One was the warlike Sioux. Another was the Sauk. These and other tribes, including the Fox, Iowa, and Winnebago, occupied most of the state until the 1800s.

Iowa was a small part of the huge French territory called Louisiana. France let Spain control the Louisiana Territory for a time. But the people who entered the Iowa region during the 1700s were French.

The first one to start a settlement was Julien Dubuque, a French-Canadian pioneer from Quebec. He asked the Fox Native Americans to let him mine near the Mississippi. The chiefs granted this request in 1788. Dubuque and the Native Americans became good friends.

STATE SYMBOLS

◄ The oak, chosen as state tree in 1961, grows in almost all Iowa's woodland.

► The wild rose was adopted as Iowa's state flower in 1897.

► The eastern goldfinch, the state's bird, is also called the wild canary.

◄ The state seal for Iowa shows a soldier holding the American flag. He is surrounded by symbols of agriculture.

IOWA

Capital and largest city
Des Moines
(193,187 people)

Area
56,290 square miles
(145,780 sq. km)
Rank: 25th

Population
2,776,755 people
Rank: 30th

Statehood
December 28, 1846
(29th state admitted)

Principle river
Des Moines River

Highest point
Ocheyedan Mound
1,670 feet (509 m)

Motto
Our liberties we prize and our rights we will maintain

Song
"Song of Iowa"

Famous people
James K. Van Allen, Buffalo Bill Cody, Herbert Hoover, Henry Wallace, Meredith Wilson, Grant Wood

Spirit L.
Okoboji Lakes
Spencer
Clear L.
Mason City
Decorah
Mississippi R.
Sioux City
Fort Dodge
Cedar Falls
Waterloo
Wapsipinicon R.
Dubuque
Little Sioux R.
Missouri R.
Des Moines R.
Cedar R.
Carroll
Raccoon R.
Ames
Marshalltown
Iowa R.
Cedar Rapids
Clinton
Boyer R.
Ankeny
Newton
Coralville L.
Iowa City
Davenport
Bettendorf
West Des Moines
⊛ Des Moines
Council Bluffs
Indianola
Red Rock L.
Skunk R.
Oskaloosa
Des Moines R.
Creston
Chariton R.
Rathbun L.
Ottumwa
Fairfield
Skunk R.
Burlington R.
Keokuk
Mississippi R.

N W E S

0   50   100 Miles
0   50   100   150 Kilometers
© 1994 GeoSystems, an R.R. Donnelley & Sons Company

◄ Des Moines has been Iowa's state capital since 1857. Today, its main business activities are in the areas of wholesaling, retailing, and insurance.

1387

▲ Introduced from China and Japan in the 1800s, soybeans provide a valuable cash crop for Iowan farmers. Iowa is one of the U.S.'s biggest farming states, with farms covering about 93 percent of the state.

Almost 80,000 Iowans fought in the Civil War, and about 13,000 of them were killed.

There are about 20,000 mosques (Muslim churches) in Iran.

Today, a city and a county in Iowa have his name. They mark the place where his trading post, farm, and mines were once located.

The United States bought the whole territory of Louisiana from France in 1803. Americans found, as the French had, that the Iowa region was rich in fur-bearing animals. The American Fur Company started trading posts there to buy furs from the Native Americans. Keokuk (in Iowa's southwestern corner) is one of several towns that began as trading posts.

The Native Americans liked traders who treated them fairly. They liked being able to exchange furs for wool blankets and other goods. But some settlers cheated the Native Americans to get their land. For this reason, a number of tribes sided with Great Britain in the War of 1812. Their leader was Black Hawk, a Sauk chief. Black Hawk made peace with the white Americans after the war. But unjust treatment led him to fight them again in the Black Hawk War of 1832. He was defeated. During the years that followed, almost all the Native Americans were pushed out of Iowa.

Iowa became a state in 1846. By this time, a flood of settlers was pouring in. They came by wagon from the East and South. Most of them had oxen. They had heard that horses and mules weren't strong enough to pull plows through the thick prairie *sod* (grass-covered earth). The early farmers there became known as *sodbusters*.

Once the *sod* was broken, all was well. The farmers then had excellent cropland. News of the fertile soil spread around the world. Many European farmers came to Iowa. Most came from Germany, Norway, Sweden, Denmark, the Netherlands, and Ireland. The Amanites, a religious group from Germany, founded seven villages near Iowa City in 1855. Some of the villagers there still produce old German handicrafts. Many Dutch families settled in Pella in southeastern Iowa. Their descendants dress up in traditional Dutch costumes each spring for the annual Tulip Festival. Historical museums in Decorah, in the northeast, show how the early Norwegian farm families of this region lived and worked.

Working in Iowa

Iowa is an important farming state. Agriculture brings the state more than $10 billion of business every year. Only California and Texas earn more from their agricultural products. Iowa is the nation's leading producer of corn. Soybeans are important, too. But livestock brings in more money than crops do. Not very much corn is sold. The farmers who raise it feed it to their hogs and cattle instead.

Although Iowa is a leading agricultural state, it is also a manufacturing state. Machinery is the number-one product of Iowa's manufacturing industry. Much of it is farm machinery. Food products are second in value. Both agricultural and industrial products are exhibited at the Iowa State Fair, held in Des Moines every summer.

▶▶▶▶ **FIND OUT MORE** ◀◀◀◀
Great Lakes; Louisiana Purchase; Prairie

 IRAN

Iran is about four times the size of California and has more than one-and-a-half times as many people. Many Iranians are farmers, living in mountain villages. Others live and work in large cities, where modern buildings stand next to old mud-walled houses and *mosques* (Muslim places of worship). Wandering tribes in the deserts and mountains herd goats, sheep, and camels, whose wool and hair are used to make the

famous Persian carpets. Most Iranians are Muslims.

Iran's northern boundaries are Armenia, Azerbaijan, Turkmenistan and the Caspian Sea. The Gulf of Oman and the Persian Gulf lap its southern shores. Iraq and Turkey lie to the west, and Afghanistan and Pakistan lie to the east. Tehran, the largest city, is the capital.

Iran is mainly a plateau, 4,000 feet (1,219 m) above sea level, surrounded by mountain ranges. A vast desert stretches about 800 miles (1,300 km) across the central part of the country. Much of Iran receives 10 inches (25 cm) or less of rainfall a year. However, the area near the Caspian Sea receives up to 50 inches (127 cm).

Most of the land suitable for farming is irrigated. Wheat, barley, and rice are grown. Other crops are tobacco, tea, dates, apricots, sugar beets, cotton, and corn. The country has coal, lead, copper, chromite, and iron. However, oil is Iran's most important natural resource.

The country's industries depend upon agricultural production and natural resources. Silk, cotton, and wool are woven. Hides, tobacco, and sugar beets are processed. Oil is refined, and copper is smelted.

The Iranians are descendants of the Medes and Persians. These people came to the region about 900 years before the birth of Christ. Cyrus the Great, an ancient Persian statesman and warrior, conquered the Medes and Persians in about 550 B.C. He united the area now called the Middle East and built it into the Persian Empire.

Alexander the Great, a Greek general, conquered the Persian Empire in 331 B.C. Other invaders came and went, including Arabs, Mongols, and Turks. Britain and Russia also fought to control Iran during the 1800s.

Riza Shah Pahlavi ruled Iran as *shah* (king) from 1925 to 1941. He made reforms in transportation, government, industry, education, and the army. He demanded that parliament pass new laws, including voting rights for women. He *abdicated* (gave up the throne) in favor of his son, Mohammed Riza Pahlavi, who tried to make Iran a military power. He was deposed in 1979 by a revolution under the religious leader Ayatollah Khomeini, who set up an Islamic republic. In 1980, an eight-year war with neighboring Iraq began. Khomeini died in 1989, and the moderate, Rafsanjani was elected president.

▶▶▶▶ **FIND OUT MORE** ◀◀◀◀
Alexander the Great; Islam;
Middle East; Persia

IRAN

Capital city
Tehran
(6,043,000 people)

Area
636,296 square miles
(1,648,000 sq. km)

Population
56,923,000 people

Government
Islamic republic

Natural resources
Oil, gas, iron ore, coal, lead, chromium, copper, manganese, sulfur, zinc

Export products
Oil and oil products, natural gas, carpets, fruits, nuts, hides

Unit of money
Rial

Official language
Farsi (Persian)

© 1994 GeoSystems, an R.R. Donnelley & Sons Company

IRAQ

Capital city
Baghdad
(3,845,000 people)

Area
167,925 square miles
(434,924 sq. km)

Population
17,754,000 people

Government
One-party republic

Natural resources
Oil, natural gas, sulfur,
phosphates

Export products
Oil, dates, barley

Unit of money
Dinar

Official language
Arabic

IRAQ

The word "Iraq" comes from an Arabic word for "origin." The fertile valley between the Tigris and Euphrates rivers may have been the birthplace of civilization. Iraq is bounded by Turkey, Iran, Kuwait, Saudi Arabia, Syria and Jordan. It only has a narrow strip of coast, on the Persian Gulf. The ancient city of Baghdad is the capital.

Iraq has a varied climate. In the north, the winters are cold and the summers cool. The central area has short, cool winters and long, hot summers. Iraq receives 10 inches (25 cm) of rainfall or less a year.

About 95 percent of the Iraqi people are Muslims. Many live in and around cities, working in businesses and factories. Others are farmers and herders in small villages and towns. Some *nomadic* (wandering) shepherds live in the deserts and mountains. Their leaders, called *sheiks*, are sometimes wealthy and powerful.

Iraq's most valuable natural resource is oil. Natural gas, sulfur, gypsum, and salt are found in abundance, too. Iraq grows cotton, tobacco, fruits and grains; it is a leading producer of dates. It produces glass, cigarettes, vegetable oils, soap, woolen textiles, brick and tile.

Records of civilization in Mesopotamia go back 6,000 years. The area was conquered by Persia in 538 B.C., then invaded by several conquerors. It was under Turkish rule from 1638 to 1918, when it came under British control until its independence in 1932. Iraq has had a military government since 1968. A revolt by the northern Muslim group, the Kurds, was crushed in 1975.

President Saddam Hussein took power in 1979 and fought an eight-year war against Iran for the control of the waterway between the two countries. In 1990, Iraq invaded and annexed the tiny neighboring kingdom, Kuwait. The United Nations resolved to liberate Kuwait. Iraq refused to comply with UN resolutions, and the Persian Gulf War began in January 1991. At the end of February 1991, the United Nations forces announced that Iraq had been defeated and Kuwait was free again.

▶▶▶▶ **FIND OUT MORE** ◀◀◀◀
Islam; Kuwait; Mesopotamia; Middle East; Persian Gulf War; Tigris and Euphrates Rivers

IRELAND

Ireland is a land of wild seacoasts and misty rolling hills—so green that it is sometimes called the "Emerald Isle." Whitewashed cottages with thatched roofs dot the countryside. The Irish people are known for their wit, imagination, spirit, and hospitality.

Ireland lies west of Great Britain,

© 1994 GeoSystems, an R.R. Donnelley & Sons Company

between the Irish Sea and the Atlantic Ocean. The island is divided into two parts. Most of the island is the independent *Republic of Ireland*, often known as *Eire* (the Irish name for the whole island). The northeastern region, Northern Ireland (Ulster), is part of the *United Kingdom*. The capital of the Republic is the ancient city of Dublin.

A gentle region of hills, *loughs* (lakes), and rivers stretches across central Ireland to the west coast. Here, massive granite cliffs and rugged headlands face the storms of the Atlantic Ocean. The Shannon River, the longest river in the British Isles, flows southward across central Ireland. The climate of the island is moderate and rainy.

The Irish people are descended mainly from Celtic tribes that settled in Ireland more than 2,000 years ago. The Irish encourage the use of the ancient Celtic language, *Gaelic*.

Most people also speak English, which is spoken with an accent called a *brogue*. The major religion in Ireland is Roman Catholic.

Ireland has few natural resources. Farming and food processing are the most important industries. Tourism is a major source of income for the country, too. Visitors love the friendly people, good fishing, quaint countryside, and ancient castles. Irish dairy products, woolen goods, *stout* (a heavy, dark beer), and whiskey are exported to other parts of the world. Some rural homes and small industries in Ireland burn *peat* (a soft form of coal) from the Irish bogs for fuel. Peat diggers, with their ponies and carts, and farmers with their donkeys are familiar sights.

Saint Patrick, the patron saint of

IRELAND

Capital city
Dublin (921,000 people)

Area
27,137 square miles
(70,284 sq. km)

Population
3,509,000 people

Government
Constitutional republic

Natural resources
Zinc, natural gas, crude oil, lead, limestone, coal, peat, silver

Export products
Live animals, animal products, data processing equipment, industrial machinery

Unit of money
Punt (pound)

Official languages
English and Irish Gaelic

About one-seventh of the whole surface of Ireland is covered by *bogs*—places where peat has been formed or is now forming. *Peat* is a spongy mass of vegetable matter that is found in layers many feet thick. It is said that an inch or two of peat forms every year in Ireland's bogs. When it is dried, peat can be burned as fuel.

▶ A fishing village in County Cork on the south coast of Ireland. Much of the economy of the Republic of Ireland is based on farming and fishing.

▶ The potato was a staple food for many Irish people. During the potato famine of the 1840s, many people starved to death or were forced to emigrate.

▼ Founded in both the U.S. and Ireland, the Fenian Brotherhood supported an Irish republic. Their exploits, such as this ambush of a police van in 1867, drew attention to Irish discontent and the need to find a solution to Ireland's problems.

Ireland, converted the Irish to Christianity in the 400s. After the barbarians overran Europe in the 500s and 600s, devout Irish monks kept Christianity alive. They copied down the religious scriptures by hand in beautifully decorated books, such as the famous *Book of Kells*. Ancient Celtic folklore survived in ballads and legends. Later, Irish writers sometimes used these legends as themes for their stories and poems. Many modern Irish authors, including William Butler Yeats, James Joyce, Oscar Wilde, and George Bernard Shaw, have become famous throughout the world.

The high kings of Ireland ruled from a great palace at Tara, near Dublin, in the Middle Ages. In the 1100s, the first English invasions began from the east. In the 1500s,

English settlers began to seize land throughout Ireland. These Protestant settlers brutally persecuted the Roman Catholic Irish. The Irish had no political rights and were forced to live in poverty on the poorest land. Their diet was mainly potatoes. In the 1840s, a disease destroyed the potato crop for several years and millions of Irish people died of starvation. Others emigrated to the United States.

In 1916, a revolution known as the Easter Rebellion broke out. It was led by a group of Irish patriots called the *Sinn Féin* ("We Ourselves"). In 1949, Britain finally recognized the independence of the Republic of Ireland but kept control of the heavily Protestant northern counties. Conflict in the north between Irish nationalists and Unionists, who want the north to stay part of Britain, has led to much bloodshed. In 1985, the Republic and Britain tried to solve the problems in the north by agreeing to set up a joint commission to give the Republic an advisory role in ruling the north. But the Unionists strongly opposed this plan, and the turmoil continues in Northern Ireland.

▶▶▶▶ **FIND OUT MORE** ◀◀◀◀
British Isles; England; English History; United Kingdom

IRON AGE

The early history of the world is sometimes divided into three different periods, known as ages. These periods take their names from the materials that people used to make tools and weapons.

The Stone Age was the first great age, during which humans began to carve stones into axes, arrowheads, and other weapons. The Bronze Age followed the Stone Age in most parts of the world. People heated copper and tin to create the alloy bronze, which could be bent and hammered into many shapes. Societies were able to develop even further during the Iron Age.

Because societies developed at different rates around the world, these terms describe different periods of time. For example, some stone tools found in Africa are nearly a million years old. But some remote tribes in Asia were using stone tools well into this century. And Native Americans in the 1800s fought the U.S. Cavalry using Stone Age arrows. Other cultures had no real Bronze Age, learning ironmaking techniques while still using stone tools.

The earliest evidence of the Iron Age comes from the Middle East, in part of what is now Turkey. Sometime between 1500 B.C. and 1000 B.C., an ancient group of people known as the Hittites developed a way of smelting iron ore. That process involved heating the ore to a very high temperature until the metal could be extracted. There is evidence that people in India and China made the same discovery at about that time.

The technique of ironmaking spread quickly and allowed new societies to develop in the Middle East, Africa, Asia, and Europe. Why?

One of the main reasons was the strength of the new metal. Bronze was not strong enough to be used to make good plows. Iron, on the other hand, was ideal. With new iron plows able to till more land, many people were able to do jobs other than farming. Until then, most people were either farmers, hunters, or warriors. During the Iron Age, fewer farmers were needed to provide the food for growing populations. People began to study different subjects, to develop rules and laws, and to build larger cities. And the iron itself formed the basis of more complicated tools, weapons, coins, and utensils.

We are still touched by the advances made by those Iron Age cultures, such as those in ancient Greece and Rome. One of the greatest gifts passed down from that period is scientific curiosity. Iron Age people saw how their societies had developed by using new ideas. If using iron made life easier than using bronze, then there might be something better even than iron.

That curiosity is something that we now take for granted, as new technologies replace old ones. We still use iron, but it is now just one of hundreds of materials used to make life more comfortable and interesting.

▶ ▶ ▶ ▶ **FIND OUT MORE** ◀ ◀ ◀ ◀
Bronze Age; Iron and Steel;
Stone Age

▲ Methods of iron smelting were developed in Africa after about 500 B.C. Here, bellows are used to heat a furnace built of earth.

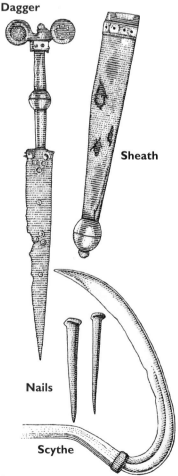

Dagger

Sheath

Nails

Scythe

▲ Iron Age tools: a Roman scythe, nails, and a Celtic dagger and sheath.

▲ Iron working began around the 600s B.C. in China. Here they are casting iron into large molds.

Have you ever wondered why iron turns red when it is heated? When it is heated to about 1500°F (800°C), the atoms in the iron vibrate and send out waves that we see as a dull red. As the temperature increases, the atoms vibrate faster and the iron turns bright red and finally white-hot before it begins to melt.

IRON AND STEEL

Thousands of years ago, people used tools made of stone, copper, or bronze. Then people began to find pieces of iron meteorites. They discovered that the iron was heavier and harder than stone, copper, or bronze. By hammering the iron, they could shape it into knives, arrowheads, and spear points, and it could even be made into jewelry. The iron was believed to have magic powers because it came from the heavens. In some ancient languages, the word for iron meant "metal from the sky." Iron was considered more valuable than gold, silver, copper, or bronze.

Copper, gold, silver, and some other metals were obtained when people learned that rocks of certain ores, or colors, were changed by fire. Fire caused the metal ore in the rocks to melt. The melting of ore to obtain metal is called smelting. The metals were poured off and cooled so they would harden. Then the hardened metals were made into tools.

No one knows exactly when or where people first discovered that they could make iron by smelting iron ore. The discovery was probably made in several different areas. The Bible mentions iron and other metals. Iron was used in China, Egypt, the Middle East, and Europe long before the time of Christ.

After it was discovered in large quantities, iron was no longer considered as valuable as some of the rarer metals. Iron ore is now mined in most countries of the world. One of the largest iron ore regions in the United States is in Minnesota, near Lake Superior. Most of the high-grade ore has been mined, but a method has been developed to process a low-grade ore called taconite.

The iron mines in Minnesota are open-pit mines. This type of mine is used when the ore is near the surface of the ground. Big loads of ore are scooped up from the open ground by giant steam shovels, to be hauled away for smelting. This digging makes a huge open pit. In other iron ore ranges, the ore is sometimes deep underground. A tunnel, or shaft, is dug downward into the ground until the ore is reached. Miners go down into the shaft and dig out the ore, which is then hoisted to the surface.

For many years, iron ore was smelted on a fire of charcoal. The iron had to be hammered and reheated several times before it was free of impurities (the other materials in the ore). The first blast furnaces were made in Europe in the 1300s. A blast furnace is a tall, cylinder-shaped building with a hearth inside on which the iron ore is smelted. Modern blast furnaces may be more than 200 feet (60 m) high. Blasts of heated air make the fire so hot that most of the impurities are burned away. The melted iron sinks to the bottom of the furnace and the impurities are collected as slag or burned off as gases. In the 1700s, people discovered that coke (a by-product of coal) smelted iron much faster than charcoal. Coke has been used for smelting ever since. Crushed limestone is also added to the fire in a

◀ The Coalbrookdale Iron-works, England, painted in 1805. The first cast-iron bridge was built at Coalbrookdale in 1779.

blast furnace. Chemicals in the limestone help to purify the iron. After the iron has been smelted in a blast furnace, it is poured into bar-shaped *pigs*, or molds. It then hardens into *pig iron*. The pigs are shipped to a *foundry*, where they are reheated and *cast* (poured into molds) to make iron products. This type of iron is called *cast iron*. Cast iron is brittle, hard, and heavy.

To make a different kind of iron, the pigs are reheated and mixed with a glasslike sand. The iron is then cooled. After it hardens, it can be put between rollers and squeezed into desired sizes. This kind of iron is called *wrought iron*. It can be bent or twisted without breaking. Wrought iron is used to make such things as iron gates, garden furniture, and pipelines.

In the 1850s, different discoveries made by three men, working separately, showed how iron could be cheaply and easily made into *steel*. The men were William Kelley, an American, Robert F. Mushet, a Scot, and Sir Henry Bessemer, an Englishman. Their inventions created the steel industry.

Steel is an *alloy* (a mixture of two or more metals). Steel is made by mixing melted iron with measured amounts of other substances, such as carbon, manganese, chromium, tungsten, molybdenum, and nickel. Different alloys make different kinds of steel. For example, *stainless steel* is mostly an alloy of iron and chromium. But all steel begins with iron ore. Steel is much stronger than iron and can be shaped more accurately.

Today, an increasingly important way of smelting iron ore is in the electric furnace. Long carbon rods, or *electrodes*, able to carry large electric currents, are lowered into a chamber containing the iron ore and limestone. They are positioned

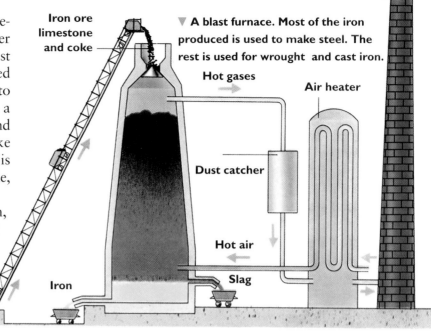

Iron ore limestone and coke

▼ A blast furnace. Most of the iron produced is used to make steel. The rest is used for wrought and cast iron.

Hot gases

Air heater

Dust catcher

Hot air

Iron

Slag

within a few inches of the ore. When the power is turned on, an electric arc jumps across the air gap. This creates intense heat that melts the metal and burns out the impurities. The quality of the steel produced is easier to control with this method.

The spray process of steelmaking is a method still in the experimental stages. In this process, molten pig iron is sprayed through a current of oxygen and a spray of limestone powder. Impurities are burned out or combined with the limestone.

The former Soviet Union, Brazil, Japan, Australia, the United States, China, and India are the world's leading producers of iron and steel. Great quantities of this iron and steel are sold to other countries that do not have enough iron mines or steel mills to meet their own needs. Iron and steel are used in the building of skyscrapers, automobiles, ships, airplanes, rockets and space ships, bicycles, railroad tracks, trains, toys, computers, knives, guns, and thousands of other goods. The iron and steel industries are among the most important industries in the world.

▶ ▶ ▶ ▶ **FIND OUT MORE** ◀ ◀ ◀ ◀
Alloy; Industrial Revolution; Iron Age; Metal; Mines and Mining

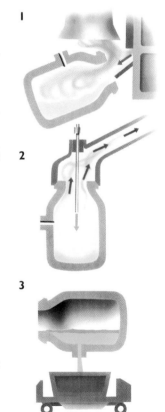

1

2

3

▲ Making steel: 1. The vessel is tilted and loaded with scrap iron and other metals. 2. It returns to upright as oxygen is blown in to "burn off" any unwanted carbon. 3. The molten steel is then poured off into molds.

▲ The Iroquois called themselves *Ongwanonhsioni,* which means "long house builders." Iroquois villages used to line the shores of lakes Erie and Ontario.

▲ Wooden masks represented mythological beings and were worn during Iroquois tribal ceremonies.

▶ Some of the first people to use irrigation were the ancient Egyptians who, by 3000 B.C., had an elaborate system of canals leading from the Nile River. Here a *shaduf* is used to raise water. A weight on one end of the pole balances the water-filled leather bucket.

IROQUOIS

In part of what is now New York State, five Native American tribes (the Mohawk, Cayuga, Seneca, Oneida, and Onondaga) united to form the Iroquois League, or the "Five Nations" before the 1600s. After 1722, they were joined by the Tuscarora and became the Six Nations. The life of the Iroquois was highly organized and culturally advanced.

The Iroquois lived in villages defended by *palisade fences,* or fences of tall, pointed pieces of wood tied closely together. They lived in long wooden structures called "long houses." Several related families lived in each house. Each family had its own part of the long house.

The Iroquois grew corn (*maize*), squash, and beans. The women of the tribes tended the fields and picked wild fruits and vegetables. Maple sugar was also enjoyed by the Iroquois. Collected elm bark was used for covering the walls and roofs of the long houses and for making containers. The men and boys went on hunting and fishing expeditions.

Women had a very important place among the Iroquois. The head of each family was an older woman. Women owned the long houses, the fields, and the crops. An Iroquois traced his or her ancestors through the mother's family. The women at the head of the most important Iroquois families chose the *sachems,* or chiefs, who sat in the tribal council. The sachems governed the tribes, but if they did not govern wisely, the women dismissed them.

Ceremonies honoring the Great Spirit were important to Iroquois life. The major ceremonies were supposed to encourage the growth of the new year's crops. The members of the False Face Society danced, wearing frightening masks. Each member carved his mask from a living tree. These masks were believed to heal the sick and destroy evil spirits.

The Iroquois believed in justice, healthy living, cooperation, and mutual respect.

▶▶▶▶ **FIND OUT MORE** ◀◀◀◀
Five Nations

IRRIGATION

For thousands of years, farmers have taken water from rivers to make up for lack of rain. At first, farmers simply dug narrow channels from the river to their fields. This was irrigation, but it had limitations. The irrigated fields had to be downhill from the river and close to it, because there were no pumps to carry the water uphill or over long distances. These problems have been solved by modern irrigation methods.

Irrigation plays an important part in agriculture today. In the United States, irrigation makes it possible for farmers to use about 40 million acres (16 million hectares) of land normally too dry for farming. The Columbia, Sacramento, San Joaquin, and Missouri rivers supply water for some of the largest irrigation systems in the United States. Other large systems are along the Nile River in

Egypt, the Hwang He River in China, the Indus River in Pakistan, the Ganges and Brahmaputra rivers in India, and the Tigris and Euphrates rivers in Iraq.

The pumps of a modern irrigation system can move millions of gallons of water a day. Some irrigation systems take water from underground wells. But most systems get water from rivers. Usually, a dam is built and the water is taken from the lake formed behind the dam.

Pumps carry water from the river into canals or concrete channels. Special tunnels are dug to carry the water under hills and mountains. Along the way are pumping stations that keep the water moving over long distances. Smaller canals, called *feeders*, branch off from the main canal, and *laterals*, still smaller canals, branch off from the feeders.

There are several ways of bringing water to the growing plants. Water may be allowed to flow from the laterals by gravity through the plowed furrows in which the crops are growing. In *underbedding*, the plants are grown on rows of small hills, and the water flows along the rows. The water seeps down to the roots of the plants.

Rows of sprinklers may be built in a field. The water is pumped through them from a central source and feeds the crops.

▶ ▶ ▶ ▶ **FIND OUT MORE** ◀ ◀ ◀ ◀
Agriculture; Canal; Dam; Pump

IRVING, WASHINGTON (1783–1859)

Washington Irving has been called the "Father of American Literature." He was the first important fiction writer in the United States and one of the first American authors to use the short-story form. His humorous stories and other writings won him fame in Europe as well as at home.

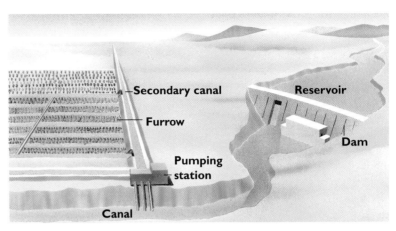

Irving was born in New York City. As a young man, he began a career as a lawyer. But he preferred writing, and soon began to publish articles and essays. He published a humorous *History of New York* in 1809, under the made-up name Diedrich Knickerbocker. This book poked fun at history and at American government.

Irving traveled to Europe in 1815 for his family's business. Money troubles caused the business to fail a few years later, and Irving turned to writing as a full-time occupation. His next work was *The Sketch Book*, which included his two most popular stories, "The Legend of Sleepy Hollow" and "Rip Van Winkle." Both of these stories were based on old legends that Irving had heard from Dutch-Americans in New York. "The Legend of Sleepy Hollow" is the tale of a timid schoolmaster, Ichabod Crane, and his terrifying meeting with the Headless Horseman. "Rip Van Winkle" is the story of a man who falls asleep for 20 years in the Catskill Mountains of New York. He wakes up after the Revolutionary War and finds that life in his town has changed completely.

Irving was appointed U.S. minister to Spain and was sent to Madrid in 1826. There he wrote several books, including a biography of Columbus. He later served as a diplomat in England, and again in Spain. He returned to America in 1846 and retired to Sunnyside, his home on the Hudson River in Tarrytown, New York.

▲ Irrigation schemes and hydroelectric power stations may both make use of water from a reservoir. Water is pumped from the river into secondary canals. Narrow ditches called "furrows" branch off from this canal at right angles to carry water between rows of crops.

▲ Washington Irving, writer and traveler, whose stories are read today in many parts of the world.

ISABELLA AND FERDINAND

Spain became a strong nation under the rule of Queen Isabella (1451– 1504) and King Ferdinand (1452– 1516). In the early 1400s, Spain was a group of kingdoms. In 1469, at the age of 17, Ferdinand of

▼ It took nearly six years for Queen Isabella of Spain to agree to support Columbus' voyage to find a passage west to reach China and India.

▶ The symbol of Islam is the crescent moon and star. It often appears on the flags of Muslim countries.

▲ An Islamic mosque with four *minarets* or towers from which the *muezzin* announces prayers five times a day.

the kingdom of Aragon married Isabella of Castile. She was just 18. Their marriage combined the two largest kingdoms in Spain. Isabella was a strong queen. She wanted to drive the Moors out of Spain. The Moors were Arabs who had come over to Spain from Africa. The *Moors* were forced to give up their last stronghold in the south, Granada, in 1492. In that same year, Isabella and Ferdinand gave Christopher Columbus the money he needed to make his first voyage in search of a westward route to India.

Isabella and Ferdinand wanted all of Spain to be Roman Catholic. They supported the *Inquisition*—special courts that tried anyone suspected of not believing the teachings of the Roman Catholic Church.

Ferdinand was a good soldier and good at negotiating with other lead-

ers. He brought all the land south of the Pyrenees Mountains, except Portugal, under the control of Spain. He also conquered Naples in Italy, and the islands of Corsica and Sardinia.

▶▶▶▶ **FIND OUT MORE** ◀◀◀◀
Columbus, Christopher; Spain; Spanish History

ISLAM

Islam is one of the world's great religions. Its greatest *prophet* (religious proclaimer) was Muhammad, an Arab who lived from about A.D. 570 to 632. People who believe in Islam are called *Muslims*. Today, there are almost 600 million Muslims throughout the world. Most of them live in the Middle East, Africa, and Asia.

Islam in Arabic means "peace, purity, and obedience to God." According to Muslim belief, Muhammad saw the angel Gabriel in a vision. Gabriel told Muhammad that he was to be God's messenger to teach the words of God to the world. Those words became the holy writings of Islam, the book called the *Koran*.

Muhammad lived in Mecca, a great Arabian trading city. At that time, the Arab tribes worshiped many gods. Muhammad preached that there was only one God. He urged the people to give up their wicked ways and live virtuous lives. The people of Mecca did not wish to change their ways and persecuted Muhammad. The prophet fled to another city, Medina, in A.D. 622. His flight, called the *Hegira*, is holy to Islam. Muslims date their calendar from this year. In Medina, Muhammad became a powerful leader. Before his death, the people living in Mecca became Muslims, too.

After Muhammad died, belief in Islam continued to spread. Its Arab

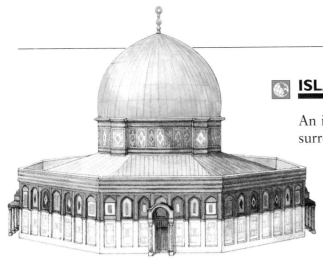

▲ **The Dome of the Rock in Jerusalem is the third most important Muslim shrine after Mecca and Medina.**

followers (called *Moors* in North Africa and Spain) carved out an empire. They conquered Persia, Syria, and Egypt, and invaded Spain and France. However, internal struggles for power and European opposition helped to break up the Muslim empire after the 1200s.

Muslims believe that "There is no god but Allah [God], and Muhammad is the prophet of Allah." They believe in the same God as Christians and Jews, and in the religious teachers of the Old Testament, such as Abraham, Isaac, and Jacob. Muslims think of Jesus Christ as a great teacher, and believe that there will be a Judgment Day when the good will go to heaven and the wicked will go to hell.

Muslims pray five times each day, always facing toward Mecca. A *muezzin*, or crier, announces prayer time from the *minaret* (tower) attached to the *mosque*, or temple. An *imam*, or chief religious official, leads the people in prayer. Every able person must give *alms* (money) to the poor. During the holy month of *Ramadan*, adult Muslims must *fast* (go without food or drink) between sunrise and sunset. Once during his lifetime, every Muslim is supposed to make a *hadj*, or visit, to the holy city of Mecca. Muslims are not supposed to drink liquor, eat pork, or gamble.

▶ ▶ ▶ ▶ **FIND OUT MORE** ◀ ◀ ◀ ◀
Koran; Mosque; Muhammad

ISLAND

An island is a body of land entirely surrounded by water. In a way, even the continents are islands because they are surrounded by oceans. Australia is often called the "island-continent." But all the continents are very large, and the word "island" is most often used to mean a smaller body of land.

In the ocean, islands may be part of a continental shelf. These islands formed at the end of the last ice age, when the level of the ocean rose and covered low-lying areas at the edges of the continents. Newfoundland, off Canada's east coast, was formed this way. So were the British Isles. Many oceanic islands, such as the Aleutian Islands, form groups called "island arcs." These are volcanic islands and occur alongside deep trenches in the ocean floor, where one *crustal plate* (a rigid portion of the Earth's crust) is slipping beneath another. The friction caused by this movement heats the rocks until they erupt as volcanoes. Many small islands are simply large circular coral reefs called *atolls*.

Islands in rivers are sandbars or areas of hard rock that have resisted the action of the water that cut the riverbed. Islands in lakes are usually higher parts of the lakebed exposed above the surface of the water.

▶ ▶ ▶ ▶ **FIND OUT MORE** ◀ ◀ ◀ ◀
Continent; Coral; Great Barrier Reef; Mountain; Plate Tectonics; Volcano

THE FIVE LARGEST ISLANDS

Greenland (N. Atlantic)
839,999 sq. miles
(2,175,429 sq. km)

New Guinea (S. Pacific)
345,054 sq. miles
(893,621 sq. km)

Borneo (Pacific)
289,859 sq. miles
(750,677 sq. km)

Madagascar (Indian)
241,094 sq. miles
(624,385 sq. km)

Baffin (N. Atlantic)
183,810 sq. miles
(476,031 sq. km)

▼ **Great Britain is the world's seventh largest island. It was created when the glaciers melted at the end of the last Ice Age. The seas rose, filling the English Channel and separating Britain from the rest of Europe.**

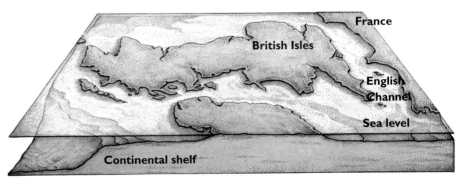

▲ The Israeli flag was raised for the first time at Elat on the Gulf of Aqaba.

▼ A group of Arabs plow the land and sow seed near the modern city of Bethlehem.

ISOTOPE

SEE ATOM

 # ISRAEL

Since the modern-day state of Israel was established in 1948, the Israeli people have changed a barren, nonproductive land into one of the most industrialized and advanced nations of the world. The Israelis have built modern towns, factories, and schools. A national irrigation project has made large parts of Israel, including the dry, rocky Negev Desert, a fertile land.

Israel is located in part of the area that was once Palestine. Ancient Israel was the traditional homeland of the Jewish people. It is also the birthplace of Christianity—the land where Jesus Christ lived. Jerusalem, the capital, is a holy city for Jews, Christians, and Muslims.

Israel is a narrow country, slightly larger than the state of New Jersey. The land in the north and east is hilly, but it is flat along the coast of the Mediterranean Sea. The Negev Desert in the southern part of the country occupies more than half of the total land area. The Jordan River Valley lies in the eastern part of the country. The lowest point of land in the world, the Dead Sea, is located there.

Israel has a warm climate throughout the year. Most of the rain falls in the winter. The northern part of the country receives more rain than the southern desert.

Israeli farmers grow much of their country's food. The principal crops include oranges and other citrus fruits, olives, barley, wheat, tomatoes, potatoes, figs, and corn. One type of farming community frequently found in Israel is the *kibbutz*. People live and work together on a kibbutz, sharing the farm equipment and the money earned from the produce.

Large factories are located in and around Haifa and Tel Aviv. The principal industrial products are chemicals, electrical equipment, plastics, tires, metal goods, pharmaceuticals, processed foods, textiles, and polished diamonds.

In the 1800s, mass killings of Jews in Russia and other parts of Eastern Europe caused thousands of Jews to emigrate to Palestine. Great Britain received control of Palestine from the League of Nations after World War I (1918). The British and the League promised to make Palestine a "national homeland" for Jews. The Arabs living in Palestine and the surrounding countries were violently against having a Jewish nation there.

Nazi persecution in the 1930s forced thousands of Jews to flee from Germany and other European countries. Many settled in Palestine. Thousands more arrived after World War II. The Palestine Arabs began to attack the Jewish settlements. In order to stop the fighting, the British announced that only a small number of Jews could enter the country. This satisfied the Arabs, but the number of Jewish immigrants kept growing. Thousands of refugees waited on ships, hoping to be admitted.

The British submitted the problem to the United Nations. The U.N. voted to divide Palestine into two separate states—one Arab and one

Jewish. The British left Palestine in 1948, and the Jewish state of Israel was formed. Many Palestinian Arabs left Israel to live in refugee camps.

Israel is a parliamentary democracy. The elected legislative body, the *Knesset*, elects the president and the prime minister. The nation has no written constitution, and authority lies with the legislature.

Since its birth, Israel has been involved in clashes with neighboring Arab states. There have been bitter disputes over the land, the water supply and the use of the Suez Canal.

In the Six-Day War of 1967, Israel captured territory from Egypt, Jordan, and Syria. Another war in 1973, between Israel and Arab countries, ended in a U.N. ceasefire resolution. In 1979, Israel signed a peace treaty with Egypt, but continued to clash with other Arab countries. Israel attacked Palestine Liberation Organization bases in Lebanon in 1982.

In 1991, Iraq's bombing of Israel during the Persian Gulf War drew attention back to the Arab-Israeli problem. In November of that year, Western diplomats persuaded Arab and Israeli leaders to meet at a peace conference in Madrid. After elections in 1992, the prime minister, Yitzhak Rabin, called for peace and reconciliation with their Arab neighbors.

▶ ▶ ▶ ▶ **FIND OUT MORE** ◀ ◀ ◀ ◀

Dead Sea; Egypt; Islam; Jerusalem; Jewish History; Jordan; Judaism; Middle East; Palestine

ITALIAN

SEE ROMANCE LANGUAGES

ITALIAN HISTORY

The Italian peninsula in Europe has a history of almost ceaseless warfare within its shores and countless invasions from abroad. For most of its history, Italy was not united as one nation.

About 1,000 years before the birth of Christ, many different tribes lived in the Italian peninsula. The most powerful were the Etruscans whose homeland was a region in central Italy. The Etruscans conquered lands to the north and south but were

ISRAEL

Capital city
Jerusalem
(458,000 people)

Area
8,019 square miles
(20,770 sq. km)

Population
4,616,000 people

Government
Multi-party republic

Natural resources
Potash, bromine, phosphates, copper, clay, sulfur, manganese

Export products
Polished diamonds, citrus and other fruits, textiles and clothing, chemicals, machinery and other manufactured goods, processed foods

Unit of money
Shekel

Official languages
Hebrew, Arabic

▲ **Nero, the Roman emperor who ruled so badly that eventually he had to flee from Rome.**

▲ **An old print of the Arsenal in Venice, where its ships were built. Trade by sea with Muslim countries brought Venice immense wealth.**

1402

never able to take over the whole peninsula.

The Italian city of Rome succeeded where the Etruscans had failed. The Roman people not only conquered the whole of Italy, but by 27 B.C., they had also created a huge empire in Europe and the Middle East. The Roman Empire prospered for about 500 years. But in the 300s, German tribes from the north began to invade the western part of the empire. The last Roman emperor of the West, Romulus Augustulus, was defeated by a German barbarian, Odoacer, in A.D. 476. From that date until the mid-1800s, Italy was for the most part divided into a group of small states. These states fought continually among themselves. They found it difficult to combine, even against a foreign invader. Italy was overrun again and again by more powerful peoples from other parts of Europe.

From about A.D. 60, Rome had been the headquarters of the pope, leader of the Roman Catholic Church. In A.D. 572, Italy was invaded by a fierce German tribe, the Lombards, who conquered many regions and threatened to attack Rome. The pope appealed for help to the most powerful ruler in Europe, the king of the Franks. Later, the Frankish king, Charlemagne, finally drove the Lombards out of Italy. He was crowned Emperor of the Romans in A.D. 800 by Pope Leo III. The Franks gave the pope a large area of land in central Italy. This area became known as the Papal States. The popes soon became strong enough to resist attempts by invaders to take over the Papal States.

After the death of Charlemagne, the Franks and the Germans struggled for control of Italy. In A.D. 962, northern Italy was captured by a powerful German king, Otto the Great. Otto was crowned Holy Roman Emperor by the pope. For

the next 500 years, Italy was dominated by the Holy Roman emperors and the popes. By this time, many Italian cities had become important trading centers. They grew wealthy and powerful, and some became self-governing states. Among the greatest of these city-states were Florence, Genoa, Milan, Pisa, and Venice. Genoa and Venice were ruled by powerful magistrates, called *doges*, who were similar to today's mayors. Wealthy merchants in the cities encouraged the work of artists and scholars. The Italian cities were the birthplace of the great movement of new ideas known as the *Renaissance*.

▲ **In Renaissance Italy many churches were built, like this one at Pavia.**

Italy was invaded by France in 1494. Shortly afterward, the Holy Roman Empire was split between Spain and Austria. For the next 400 years, Italy became a battleground for struggles among these three powers. At one point, northern Italy was united as the Kingdom of Italy by the French emperor Napoleon I. But after Napoleon's defeat at the Battle of Waterloo in 1815, Italy was once again divided among several rulers.

By the mid-1800s, the Italian people began to speak of fighting for a free and united Italy. Several revolutions were organized against the Austrians, who ruled at that time.

By 1860, Count Cavour, the prime minister of the Kingdom of Sardinia, had united most of northern Italy against Austria. The same year, the Italian patriot, Giuseppe Garibaldi, led his army of "Redshirts" to victory in southern Italy. By 1870, the whole peninsula had been united as the Kingdom of Italy. The first king was Victor Emmanuel II of Sardinia.

The long years of war left the Italian people poor and hungry. They became dissatisfied with the new government when it did very little to help them. Italy's rulers were more interested in gaining power and influence abroad. During World War I (1914–1918), Italy fought with Great Britain and France against Austria-Hungary and Germany. Italians became even poorer, and when a new leader, Benito Mussolini, promised to bring back the wealth and glory of the Roman Empire, many people supported him. Mussolini became premier of Italy in 1922. He organized a fascist government with himself as dictator. In 1936, he signed a treaty with the German dictator, Adolf Hitler. Italy, Japan, and Germany were defeated by The Allies: Britain, the U.S., and Russia in World War II (1939-1945), and Mussolini was killed by his own people.

In 1946, free elections were held in Italy. The people voted to end the monarchy, and Italy became a republic. The government began programs to improve the lives of the people. Northern Italy is now one of the most industrialized regions of Europe. But the Italian people are still split by fierce struggles between different political parties. The Communist party in Italy has become one of the largest Communist parties outside the former Soviet Union and China.

▶▶▶▶ **FIND OUT MORE** ◀◀◀◀

Charlemagne; Dictator; Etruscan; Fascism; Holy Roman Empire; Italy; Mussolini, Benito; Napoleon; Pope; Renaissance; Rome; Rome, Ancient; Venice; World War I; World War II

ITALY

Visitors like Italy for its scenic landscapes, ancient ruins, beautiful architecture, and great art museums. Tourism is an important business in this usually sunny country, well known also for its lovely beaches, lake resorts, and Alpine ski lodges.

The 700-mile (1,125-km) long Italian peninsula, shaped like a boot, extends into the Mediterranean Sea. The snowcapped Alps Mountains rise along its northern border, which is shared with France, Switzerland, and Austria. A chain of mountains, the Apennines, runs down the center of Italy. The mountains often rise from the very edge of the sea. Many of Italy's coastal towns are crowded into narrow spaces between cliffs and the sea. The Po Valley lies just south of the Alps. The Mediterranean islands of Sicily, Sardinia, Elba, Capri, and Ischia are also part of Italy.

Rome is the capital of Italy. The pope rules over Vatican City, a tiny independent church state located in the heart of Rome.

Before World War II, most Italians were farmers. After the war, many factories were built, and Italy became an important industrial nation and a member of the European Community. The most important farming and industrial area is the Po Valley. Textiles, chemicals, machinery, and automobiles are produced in factories in the valley's cities. Cattle and sheep graze in the lush pastures, and orchards produce peaches and apples. In parts of western and southern Italy, farmers grow oranges, lemons, and olives. Grapes for wine are cultivated throughout the country.

In southern Italy, the soil is poor and farming is difficult. Most rivers dry out during the hot summers. Farmers work very hard to earn a living. They often plant their crops on steep hillsides where the soil is held in place by stone walls. Most Italian farm families live in small towns.

▲ An illustration based on a nineteenth century cartoon showing Garibaldi, the Italian patriot, assisting King Victor Emmanuel II to step into the Italian "boot."

▼ The Leaning Tower of Pisa, one of Italy's best-known monuments, was completed in 1350. It leans because the ground underneath it began to sink soon after the first three stories were built.

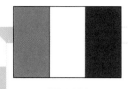

ITALY

Capital city
Rome (2,816,000 people)

Area
116,304 square miles
(301,225 sq. km)

Population
57,461,000 people

Government
Constitutional republic

Natural resources
Mercury, sulfur, marble, potash, coal, some oil and natural gas

Export products
Textiles, clothing, metals, wine, transportation equipment, chemicals, fruit, vegetables

Unit of money
Italian lira

Official language
Italian

Before 1870, Italians were not ruled by one national government. The region was a patchwork of small kingdoms, independent territories, and *Papal States* (areas governed by the pope, or Roman Catholic Church). When the country was finally united, it was ruled by King Victor Emmanuel II. Benito Mussolini, a fascist dictator, became the country's leader in 1922, although the king still reigned. Italy became a republic after World War II. Today, president, prime minister, cabinet, and parliament form the government. Italy has had many governments since World War II. Few have lasted much more than a year. Labor strikes have unsettled the country. In the 1970s and 1980s, atrocities committed by the Red Brigades, a small group of extreme leftists, and Palestinian terrorists created fear in the country.

▶▶**FIND OUT MORE**◀◀

Adriatic Sea; Fascism; Florence; Italian History; Mediterranean Sea; Mussolini, Benito; Rome; Rome, Ancient; Vatican City

IVORY COAST

SEE COTE D'IVOIRE

Italy is the world's largest producer of wine, with nearly 8 billion liters a year out of a world production of 35 billion bottles. Italians drink more wine than the people of any other nation do—more than 24 gallons (90 liters) in a year per each person in the population.

JACKAL

The jackal is a large-eared wild dog. It is generally light brownish yellow or tawny in color, with a dark tip to its tail. An adult jackal is more than 2 feet (60 cm) long and weighs about 20 pounds (10 kg), resembling a small wolf or coyote. Jackals are found in Asia, Africa, and parts of Europe. They are usually seen in pairs, but often hunt in packs of 5 to 20.

Jackals are mainly scavengers that feed on the remains of dead animals. But they also hunt small animals, such as poultry and baby antelopes. Their hunting is usually done at night, when their yapping and howling can be heard. Jackals also eat fruits and vegetables. During the day, they hide in burrows, caves, tall grass, or bushes. Sometimes jackals interbreed with domestic dogs and wolves.

The golden, or Asiatic, jackal ranges from central Asia to North Africa. Golden jackals usually hunt in packs. The side-striped jackal and black-backed jackal live in eastern and southern Africa and are mostly solitary animals. The side-striped jackal is so called because it has a pair of light and dark stripes on each side of its body.

▶ ▶ ▶ ▶ **FIND OUT MORE** ◀ ◀ ◀ ◀
Coyote; Dog; Wolf

▼ **The Arabs call the jackal the "howler" because of its mournful cry.**

JACKASS

SEE DONKEY

JACKRABBIT

RABBITS AND HARES

JACKSON, ANDREW (1767–1845)

Jackson's admirers called him "The People's President." Jackson was the first President to come from humble origins. Born a few days after his father died, young Andy had little schooling, but much courage. When he was 13, the Revolutionary War began. He joined the volunteers, but he and his brother Robert were captured by the British. A British officer ordered Andy to clean his boots, but the boy refused. The officer slashed him with a sword. The two boys were marched 40 miles (65 km) to a prison, where they caught smallpox. Andy got better, but Robert died. His mother later died of a fever, caught while caring for the wounded. Andy's only other brother had been killed earlier in the war. At the age of 14, he was left without a family.

He stayed with relatives and tried various jobs, including saddle-making and teaching. Eventually he settled on law and became a lawyer at the age of 20. In 1788, he was appointed attorney general for the area that became Tennessee, and he moved to Nashville. There, he met and married Rachel Robards. At the time of the marriage, Mrs. Robards thought that her previous husband had divorced her. But the divorce did not go through until she had been

DEVELOPMENT OF THE LETTER J

The Egyptian J
c. 3000 B.C.

The Phoenician J
c. 1000 B.C.

The Greek J
c. 600 B.C.

The Roman J
c. A.D. 600

**ANDREW JACKSON
SEVENTH PRESIDENT**

**MARCH 4,1829–
MARCH 4,1837**

Born: March 15, 1767, Waxhaw, South Carolina

Parents: Andrew and Elizabeth Hutchinson Jackson

Education: Mostly self-educated

Religion: Presbyterian

Occupation: Lawyer and army officer

Political party: Democratic (formerly the Democratic-Republican Party)

State represented: Tennessee

Married: 1791 to Rachel Donelson Robards (1767-1828)

Children: 1 adopted son

Died: June 8, 1845, The Hermitage, Nashville, Tennessee

Buried: The Hermitage, Nashville, Tennessee

▶ **Jackson's troops fought the British at the Battle of New Orleans. The War of 1812 was officially over, but word had not yet reached New Orleans.**

married to Jackson for two years. The two were remarried. But Jackson's enemies often criticized his wife. Mrs. Jackson was hurt by the attacks and avoided public life. Jackson served briefly in the House of Representatives and the Senate but returned to Tennessee in 1798 to become a judge.

Jackson became a military hero during the War of 1812. His soldiers called him "Old Hickory" because he was so tough. He led his side to victory at the Battle of New Orleans.

In 1818, Jackson led a raid on the Seminoles in Florida, which was still owned by Spain. He became the first governor of Florida after Spain sold it to the United States in 1821, but resigned after four months.

Jackson ran for President in 1824. He received more votes than the other candidates, but he did not have the necessary majority. According to the Constitution, the election was decided by the U.S. House of Representatives. They decided that John Quincy Adams should be President. Jackson ran again in 1828. This time he won and was elected President. After the inauguration, Jackson invited a crowd into the White House. In their haste to shake hands with him, the people overturned chairs and tables, broke dishes, and tore curtains. Jackson narrowly

escaped through a window.

Jackson gave many government jobs to his political associates. This was called the *spoils system* (when the winner in an election gives jobs to friends and can fire the people who previously held these jobs).

In 1832, Congress passed a bill to renew the charter of the Bank of the United States. This bank, in which government funds were deposited, was controlled by private individuals. The bank was accused of favoring rich people. Jackson *vetoed* (refused to sign) the bill. He said he was opposed "to the advancement of the few at the expense of the many." He was reelected President that year.

Jackson also took a firm stand when the South Carolina legislature voted to *nullify* (reject) an import tax law passed by Congress. The President threatened to use force, if necessary, to make sure the law was obeyed. He believed that the Union would be in danger if one state was permitted to nullify a law passed by the Federal Government. He said in his last address as President, "By every sacrifice, this Union must be preserved."

▶▶▶▶ **FIND OUT MORE** ◀◀◀◀

Adams, John Quincy; Calhoun, John C.; Clay, Henry; War of 1812

JACKSON, HELEN HUNT (1830–1885)

The American writer, Helen Hunt Jackson, became well known for her work to help Native Americans.

Born in Amherst, Massachusetts, she was a lifelong friend of the poet, Emily Dickinson. In 1852, Helen married Major E. B. Hunt, who was accidentally killed. Helen began writing poetry for magazines, using the signature "H. H.," which soon became her pen name. In 1875, she married William S. Jackson and moved to Colorado Springs, Colorado. She also wrote children's stories, novels, and travel sketches.

Since childhood, Helen Hunt Jackson had been interested in the Native Americans. Her book, *A Century of Dishonor*, published in 1881, was an historical account of the U.S. government's mistreatment of the Native Americans. Mrs. Jackson was made a special investigator to look into the condition of the Native Americans living in the missions of California.

Ramona, her romantic novel about Native American life, appeared in 1884. The story's heroine, Ramona, saw the Native Americans being driven to extinction by "civilization."

▶▶▶▶**FIND OUT MORE**◀◀◀◀
Native Americans

JACKSON, JESSE (1941–)

The Reverend Jesse Jackson is an influential political leader and spokesman for the Civil Rights movement. The hardships of his own childhood in Charleston, South Carolina, convinced him that black Americans still had to struggle to achieve the same rights enjoyed by other Americans. He has combined his political efforts with his role as a Baptist minister.

In the 1960s, Jackson became a friend and colleague of Dr. Martin Luther King Jr. Like King, Jackson urged his supporters to use nonviolent methods of protest.

In 1971, Jackson formed PUSH (People United to Save Humanity). This organization aimed to improve economic prospects for blacks.

In the 1980s, Jackson tried to earn the Democratic Party's nomination for President in 1984 and 1988, but failed. However, he is recognized as a spokesman for millions of Afro-Americans and continues to organize demonstrations promoting civil rights.

▶▶▶▶ **FIND OUT MORE** ◀◀◀◀
Black Americans; Civil Rights; Civil
Rights Movement;
King, Martin Luther Jr.

JACKSON, MAHALIA (1911–1972)

One of America's most famous gospel and concert singers was Mahalia Jackson. She was also a recording artist and a devoted civil- rights worker.

She was born in New Orleans, Louisiana, where she sang in a Baptist church choir. Mahalia also listened to the music of street singers and soon developed her own style.

At 15, Mahalia moved to Chicago, where her singing in churches and revival meetings attracted attention. She sang on radio and television and made many recordings. In 1950, she sang in Carnegie Hall, New York. Her strong contralto voice and the deep religious feeling she brought to her songs won her many admirers.

Mahalia toured abroad and appeared at American jazz festivals. She sang *spirituals*, religious folk songs handed down from generations as well as *gospel songs*, religious songs written by composers. In 1963, she sang for the marchers at Washington, D.C., to demand equal rights for blacks. She also sang at the funeral of Dr. Martin Luther King Jr. in 1968.

▲ Helen Hunt Jackson, writer and champion of the cause of Native Americans.

▲ The Rev. Jesse Jackson, political leader.

▲ Mahalia Jackson, American gospel singer.

JACKSON, THOMAS JONATHAN("STONEWALL") (1824–1863)

▲ **Stonewall Jackson, Confederate general.**

Stonewall Jackson was one of the most famous generals of the Confederate Army during the Civil War. He was born in Clarksburg, Virginia (now West Virginia). He graduated from the U.S. Military Academy, served in the Mexican War, and taught at the Virginia Military Institute for ten years.

When the Civil War began, he joined the Confederate Army. He fought in the first Battle of Bull Run at Manassas, Virginia, in July 1861. A Confederate officer said that Jackson and his soldiers stood "like a stone wall" against the heavy fire of the Union Army. The South won the battle, and Jackson became known as "Stonewall."

Serving under General Robert E. Lee, Jackson and his troops were victorious in the Shenandoah Valley, at Fredericksburg, and at the second Battle of Bull Run. Jackson became famous for the speed with which his soldiers could march from place to place. He was greatly respected by them and by his fellow officers.

In May 1863, Jackson's army helped defeat a Northern army at Chancellorsville, Virginia. But as Jackson returned from the front lines on horseback at twilight, Southern troops thought he was an enemy officer and shot him. His last words were, "Let us cross the river and rest in the shade."

▶▶▶▶ **FIND OUT MORE** ◀◀◀◀
Civil War

QUIZ ANSWERS

Horse quiz, page 1298

1. Horses belong to the Equidae family. Donkeys and zebras also belong to this same branch of the animal kingdom.
2. Equestrian is the word for horsemanship or to be on horseback that comes from the root word *equus*, meaning horse.
3. The oldest breed of saddle horse is the Arabian horse.
4. The two breeds of harness horse are the standard bred and the hackney. Both are very strong, heavy-boned horses.
5. Mustangs are wild horses, but they were once domestic. They are descended from domestic horses that escaped from their owners.

Inca quiz, page 1352

1. Cuzco was the capital city of the Inca civilization.
2. No, there are no Inca people who have survived to this day. However, their language (Quechua) is still spoken by the Peruvian Indians who live along the Andes mountain range.
3. The Incas' most important crops were potatoes and corn.
4. Machu Picchu is the name of the site of the isolated and impressive Inca town located high in the Andes.
5. The Inca government used the *quipu*, a long, knotted, fiber rope used as a sort of calculator and record-keeper, to manage and maintain control over the empire.

Industrial Revolution quiz, page 1367

1. England was the birthplace of the Industrial Revolution, for it was there, in the early 1800s, that the first factories were established.
2. The inventor James Watt developed the working steam engine in the mid-1700s. The steam engine's power made it possible to create many new industrial machines.
3. *Mass production* is the system of making great quantities of a product quickly and very inexpensively.
4. The first modern textile factory in the United States was the one set up by Francis Cabot Lowell in Waltham, Massachusetts.
5. Living and working conditions in the first factory towns were terrible. Men, women, and children had to work long hours at hard labor, and their housing was often of poor quality and even dangerous.

Insect quiz, page 1371

1. A young insect is called a nymph.
2. The insecticide DDT was banned by the U.S. government in 1972. It was banned because it was dangerous to fish and other animals, as well as to other useful insects.
3. The three parts of an insect's body are the head, thorax, and abdomen.
4. Insects breathe through their spiracles, the rows of openings that run along both sides of their bodies.
5. Yes. Spiders belong to the same Class of the animal kingdom as insects (the Insecta Class), even though they are technically part of a separate Order (the Araneida). Also, their bodies have only two (rather than three) parts and they have four pairs of legs (instead of three).

Intelligence test, page 1374

1. b 2. c 3. a 4. b 5. c.